Essays for Excellence

A collection of GCSE essays to
support students and teachers
in achieving success

Becky Jones
and Laura Webb

First Published 2022

by John Catt Educational Ltd,
15 Riduna Park, Station Road,
Melton, Woodbridge IP12 1QT

Tel: +44 (0) 1394 389850
Email: enquiries@johncatt.com
Website: www.johncatt.com

ISBN: 978 1 915261 33 5

Set and designed by John Catt Educational Limited

Contents

Introducing the collection

1 The importance of model essays

Reflection notes

1.1 A necessary tool – intent

We've all been there. The class are ready for their assessment, and you have all your ducks in a row ready to succeed. Their knowledge of the text is secure, they know what methods the writer has used, the context the text exists in, and how to write a paragraph. It has been a successful term, and as you reach the assessment, the students seem prepared. The assessment finishes, you look through their books, and your heart sinks. The responses lack quality and quantity, and in no way represent the learning that you felt confident had happened in the classroom.

This is a situation which many teachers will be familiar with and one we face often, at many stages of our careers. I once watched a trainee teacher deliver a lovely series of lessons on creative writing, exposing students to excellent writing, teaching them how to vary sentence structure and embedding vocabulary throughout the lessons. When they completed their mini-assessment, he was horrified: each student had written one single paragraph. I asked him if they knew how to use paragraphs, and the penny dropped when he realised he had only ever shown them short examples, nothing longer than a few sentences. The students were mimicking the successful exemplars he had shared with them – the problem was that these were only a few sentences long.

The most powerful tool in GCSE English Literature is to show our students high quality essays that truly show them the excellence we are aiming for. A student never fully understands what they need to achieve, or aspire to achieve, until they have seen it. We are firm believers that high expectations of students are paramount to student success in their final exams; this is true of behaviour and attitude to learning, oracy and discussion, revision and study habits – every component that makes up an excellent learning experience. But we often see that with model essays, teachers never show students what is truly possible. Perhaps it is a fear of over-pitching the lesson, scaring the students, flaunting your own abilities, or simply not having the time to write a high-level response.

However, you will never ensure students achieve excellence unless they see what excellence looks like.

No one wants students to underachieve. We have aimed to write this book with both teachers and students in mind, considering what we most need as teachers who teach students every day. We hope the essays in here will provide valuable teaching tools, an opportunity to push students to excellence, and to enhance your own subject knowledge of the texts you teach. Or, if you are a student seeking to be excellent, we hope these essays give you a standard to aim for. Most importantly, we hope that when you reach the right stage in learning, moving towards a summative assessment, your ducks will always have access to essays that will lead to excellence, regardless of whether you have the time to write them.

1.2 Finding the time – implementation

Put quite simply: schools are some of the busiest workplaces to exist. This is potentially due to the volume of individuals all found together on a relatively small footprint and also due to the fact that we are working with people – teenagers to be precise. And, as we all know, teenagers can be unpredictable. Think of that PPA on your timetable that you earmarked to complete that set of year eight books once a fortnight – how many times has that become a reality? Exactly. Schools and schedules are ever in flux and, for that reason, staff have to be flexible – we can be expected to cover a class, support a child through the heartbreak of their first love, or phone a concerned parent at the drop of a hat, which means our best laid plans rarely make it off the to-do list. This is where this book comes into its own. We recognise that even with the best intentions, sometimes finding an hour to write a model essay just feels like the most mammoth task after a day full of unexpected twists and turns. This doesn't make any of us a 'bad' or 'lazy' teacher – it just makes us human.

We openly acknowledge in our own roles that teaching is the front-line action of a school, but sometimes other tasks turn up and that hour where you wanted to map out a plan and write a couple of paragraphs for a feedback lesson doesn't come to fruition. You can't turn up to a classroom unprepared and expect it to be the smoothest lesson of the week. In this vein, you also can't magic up a model essay in ten snatched minutes at the end of break. Over the course of the last five years, we have been working hard to write essays to share with students. We share them with each other and our department as we believe that all students should have the opportunity to access them. After all, we are a team and we don't believe in creating excellent materials that only benefit our own individual classes. The workload of teachers has long been a bone of contention within the profession, yet we both stand by the fact that when you put the work in in the initial stages, the following lessons and weeks become easier. There is no need for anyone to reinvent the wheel – the essays in this book are designed to be picked up and used with your students as they are. If they inspire you to then add a paragraph that you know will help your particular class then brilliant – but we've put this collection together so that you can do what you do best – teach.

It also hasn't passed us by that education has embraced a much more rigorous approach to ensuring that the work of students is accurately awarded of late as a result of exam reform and assessment changes. Whilst this is something that we are glad of, it also doesn't come without its challenges. To conduct a worthwhile standardisation process, the material to standardise with must be present. Whilst exam boards will often provide some sample material it can be, at times, hard to translate these essays into the work that we receive in our classrooms. This collection means that instead of trying to write a set of sample essays or frantically wading through piles of student papers looking for a range of responses (a trickier task in reality than it sounds), you can rest assured that these essays will help to focus your eyes and place a real emphasis on what you are looking for in students' work whilst also leaving you unburdened to execute the task rather than trying to plan for it too.

1.3 Does it work? – Impact

The journey to effectively using model answers within the classroom is not a short one. It is important at this point to acknowledge that over the past five years, the way in which teachers discuss and deliver their curricula has drastically changed. Anecdotally, when we first arrived at our current school, there was a large focus on reading novels and much emphasis was therefore naturally placed on the study of literature. Pupils were exposed to a plethora of texts, had read a lot from the high-rise shelves in the dusty book cupboard and there were lessons timetabled purely for silent reading – we do not think we were alone in this approach. First and foremost, as English teachers, of course we love reading, and of course we want students to be exposed to great literature, but, before long this idea of reading with – as far as we could see – limited purpose – then became a sticking point for us. Were we apprehensive that the students weren't reading what could truly be described as 'great literature', or were we concerned that students were reading, but not understanding the texts, or, potentially worse, not doing anything with them? We maintain that there is a distinct difference between reading for pleasure and reading for progress. In an educational setting, surely we have a moral obligation to be teaching students the latter? This is a discussion that English departments across the country have been grappling with over the past decade.

Before we can begin to teach students how to write full essays successfully, we must show students how they can read for meaning and equip them with the tools to select evidence that supports what they believe are the main ideas in an extract or whole text. Through our curriculum development, we have ensured that there is a balanced approach to both language and literature. Within three years of being at the school, we cleared out the copies of *Holes* and *Skellig*, not because we don't think these are valuable books to children or benefit their general reading fluency, but because we felt that these were texts that students could access on their own or had accessed before arriving to us. We replaced these works with a slimmer, in terms of volume, yet weightier, in terms of content, selection of titles from *Animal Farm* to *The Speckled Band* and *Long Way Down*. Why? Because we fundamentally believed that if students in key stage three could successfully access these high-level texts with the support of an expert, then they would understand how to write clear points, select evidence to support them, and begin to experiment with writing analysis.

Alongside careful text selection, knowledge organisers were slowly designed to accompany each text and unit that we taught. This was not a short process, as it was important that teachers understood the purpose and function of these before even starting to use these with students. These knowledge organisers are used by all students of all abilities within the year groups. Whilst some may argue that the content within them is too challenging, or too prescriptive, when we set out our curriculum ethos (before these became fashionable and packaged up as 'curriculum intents') we purposefully placed emphasis on rich knowledge and the value of scholarship. Like many departments across the country, these decisions that were made were rooted in a shift in educational thinking and were influenced by schools that were leading the way in showing that excellent educational outcomes really were, and remain, accessible to all.

Within our setting, the use of model essays to exemplify excellence in the classroom has been unrivalled in its efficacy. Whilst it must be acknowledged that there are many other steps that must be taken before a model can be used effectively with students, as a strategy this has supported students of all abilities in achieving beyond what they may have believed themselves capable of doing. Since the new exam format began in 2017, we have worked to deliver a 'best guess' paper to all students in our department. Our 'best guess' strategy sees us trawl through previous examination papers, use our knowledge of the previous specifications to track patterns in questions and, finally, there's always a bit of luck involved! This has become easier as the years have progressed as we have made suggestions knowing which extracts, poems, characters, or themes have come up previously. Whilst we always tell students that this is what it says on the tin – a best guess – we see them mimicking our phrasing, borrowing pieces of analysis and linking together the same quotations as us and, thus far, students have been incredibly successful. We saw our department results rise by 20% from 2017 to 2019, and in 2019 our 4+ and 5+ results were 20% above the national averages. From a comprehensive setting, surrounded on all fronts by selective schools, these figures are something that we, and the students, are incredibly proud of. More than the headline figures are the individual stories of success; students with additional learning needs achieving a value-added score of +2, students accessing hospital education but through regular contact with their teacher achieving grade 9s, to those students who never thought that a pass and the opportunity to pursue a level 2 college course was going to be on the cards. Those are the true stories of success and the doors that such models cannot just push against, but truly open.

1.4 Why do children need models?

As with most things in education, and life itself, instructions on the page of a textbook or the whiteboard look very different when put into practice. If you have ever built a piece of flatpack furniture then you will know exactly what we mean. It's the same principle with essay writing: if students can't see how it should look then they won't know what they're hoping to achieve. Whatever your department's analytical acronym of choice may be (PETER, PEE, PEA, PEMEW, SIR, etc) until the students know exactly how the P in PETER needs to look in reality then it stays as little more than a 'P' in their minds. Most students will be able to tell you that they start with a point, and then they add their evidence but until they know how to effectively write that point and add that evidence to support the point without it feeling awkward or contrived then the acronym has little value. We would argue that having the acronym is akin to having a recipe – until you begin to put the ingredients together, you have little more than a neat stack of different food types. How many times have we googled the final image of a piece of furniture, or a completed recipe before we've truly been able to start and see where we are heading? It's exactly the same with models for students – without seeing it, they don't know how to transfer the knowledge and apply it to the task at hand.

1.5 What makes a good model essay?

There will undoubtedly be so many different responses to the question of 'what makes a good model essay', but for us, we think that a successful model essay should do the following:

- Exemplify the standard required for different grade ranges in line with exam board criteria.

- Show students how to include the evidence that they have chosen (embedding and introducing quotations).

- Include elements where all of the assessment objectives have been used so that students can begin to identify where these elements are within the writing and understand how they have been included so that they can emulate the style.

- Use challenging vocabulary and phrasing (suitable to the ability level).

- Have a balance of ideas that have been explicitly taught within lessons and include some different/more obscure ideas that pupils can grasp on to.
- Show how an argument can be used and returned to throughout a response.
- Considered use of the extract (if provided) and the whole text, to show students how to utilise each successfully.

1.6 Purposeful practice

As with any practice within the classroom, if we do not give students clear success criteria to work towards, we can expect variable results which may, or may not, meet our expectations of a given task. As such, when using model essays, we will often give students clear elements to look for. This helps to eliminate the potential for students to read through the essay and to do nothing helpful with it. We then will encourage students to select key ideas, phrases, or potentially methods that they think they could write about in their own work and then we actively look for these elements when they begin to write their own responses. Whilst this may at first appear as if we are asking students to learn snippets of essays and just simply regurgitate them, this is simply not the case. What we are doing is exposing them to high quality work that shows them the standard that they are aiming for and asking them to transpose elements of what they have been shown into their own work. There is never a time where we would ask students to learn an essay and re-write it – they would not learn how to use the skills or their knowledge independently should this be the case. Moreover, we are equipping them with the tools to write their own individual responses to questions with clear success criteria being followed so that they can use the knowledge and skills that they have been taught within the classroom to their utmost. If you think back to the opening part of this section where students only knew how to write one beautiful paragraph for creative writing – the use of model essays helps to guide students away from this trap. If all students ever produce is paragraphs, then there is a danger that that is also what they will produce when they really need a whole essay.

2 Planning responses

2.1 Selection of evidence

One of the most common questions we are asked in the classroom with regards to planning and writing responses is often about the evidence that students should use within their answers and essays. These questions come both from students themselves and their teachers. As a result of using knowledge organisers for our key texts at GCSE, all students have a common core of approximately 15 quotations that we deemed appropriate, accessible and transferable that they are required to learn. These quotations form the basis upon which most other evidence is built, but the fact remains that we selected these quotations for students to learn as we recognise the value within them. We often talk of value when selecting evidence, so, put simply, a valuable quotation to our students is one that has a key method attached to it and/or interesting words that can be analysed at word level to create a coherent point. Furthermore, these quotations are chosen because they allow students to track structural changes too: character development, theme progression, and they link to key motifs within the text. They are, in many ways, gateway quotations that unlock further knowledge and understanding of the text itself.

As is so often the case with students who are aspirational, there will be times when students will question whether using a quotation from the knowledge organiser is going to help them to secure a particular grade. This is, in part, a result of our emphasis on doing something interesting within a high level response, yet our response is always the same: yes. Yes, it is absolutely possible to attain at the highest possible level even if every other student sitting the same exam or assessment has used the same quotations as you. This is because it is what we do with the evidence in front of us that secures the grades as opposed to the quotations themselves. It goes without saying that if you choose to select a quotation with limited value then what you are able to write about it may also be limited, but this is why we support students in making the initial quotation choices by offering specific examples on the knowledge organisers that we know are applicable to a range of questions and can be accessed on a variety of levels.

It is important to note that we would not expect our most able students to only write responses using the 15 quotations from the knowledge organiser. These students are able to select evidence of their own that complements the original choices that form the core of their knowledge base. The point here on the selection of evidence is that it is what you do with said evidence; we are hopeful that you will see exemplification in the later chapters about how the same quotations can be manipulated to suit a wide range of abilities.

2.2 Why is planning necessary (and what do the exams board say)?

Without a doubt, allocating time to teach students how to plan their way through an essay is a crucial component of their success. As teachers, we know the texts well and so will find it easier to pull together a response which takes evidence from across the play or novel thus allowing us to build a coherent answer that understands how ideas change as a text progresses. Our students, however, will not know how to do this unless we teach them. This is why we build time into our teaching of a text to focus solely on this skill. In the examiner's report from June 2019 for published by AQA English Literature Paper 1, it explicitly states that:

One strength of responses this year was an increasing sense of well-constructed responses allowing students to build an argument and demonstrate their understanding of the text effectively. There is not one model approach that we are looking for, but increasingly, we are seeing essays that open with a thesis which establishes the student's response in relation to both text and the task. This structure immediately establishes some kind of overview of the whole text, which then helps to bring the various strands of the answer together rather than, for example, seeing the extract and the whole text as separate parts of a response.[1]

Whilst we acknowledge that this is just one exam board's response to the construction of a successful answer, it is clear that students who were able to establish an argument and then use evidence from across the whole text performed strongly. This is something which can really only be achieved when students are able to plan an appropriate viewpoint in response to the question and then support it with evidence and ideas taken from across the text; this is something that they need to be taught how to do.

2.3 Planning for all students

All students can learn how to effectively plan a response and this is true for all subjects that require longer written responses, not just English! The trick to making this skill work for all is finding out which style works best for different students. As such, we advocate teaching a range of styles and supporting students in making their own decisions. In short, it doesn't matter so much which planning style is adopted, more that they actually write a plan and then use it! It is worth noting, therefore, that planning needs to be taught across the whole GCSE course and is not something that we can leave until revision kicks in. Leaving it this late means that students will not have had time to employ their chosen planning technique in mock exams or in-class assessments. As soon as we feel that a class has enough security within a text to build an analytical response (this may be something as narrow as 'explore how Scrooge is presented within stave one'), we would begin to teach planning styles before students even attempted to write a response to the question. As with anything, the more that the students are exposed to planning and understand that it is part of the process, the more it becomes second nature to them and they are more likely to use the skill when they most need it. I referred earlier to the idea that once students have made a plan then they also need to be using it and this is something that needs to be actively checked when providing feedback to students in the initial stages. Asking the questions

    a. Have you written a plan?

    b. Does your response use and follow the plan?

---

1   www.bit.ly/38z9IXy (p. 6)

are good places to start when encouraging students to reflect on their initial uses of planning (alongside a hefty dose of praise when done successfully and without prompting).

2.4 Planning styles

How to plan can be quite a personal thing from teacher to teacher and for this reason we do not have a standard planning form that all members of our department use. Instead, we actively reflect on whether the styles we have taught are working for our students and will often vary the default planning style we use depending on the needs of different classes. Throughout this book, we have used one plan for multiple responses, and used a variety of plan types, so that they form part of the model responses.

2.4.1 Anchor planning

We first came across the idea of the anchor metaphor when Alex Quigley spoke about it at the Team English National Conference in 2018 where he spoke to us about selecting a key moment from *Romeo and Juliet* to answer a specific question and then dropping the anchor at other places both before and after the first selected moment. This idea was entirely new to us when Quigley spoke of it, but the metaphor has subsequently been successful with students as they are able to understand that in order to be successful, they must find at least three different moments, scenes, or chapters and ensure that they are spread out across the length of the text. This helps with the idea of an overall response which takes into consideration how ideas, themes or characters progress which also secures that structural awareness for students which they can sometimes struggle with.

Anchor planning works particularly well when responding to questions that require students to respond to an extract as well as a whole text as the extract can often form their initial anchoring moment from which they can then select other points from the text that come before and after for that whole text overview. When using the extract as an anchor point, it is also worth thinking about plotting three points onto the plan; beginning, middle and end. Therefore, if the extract comes from the start of the text, students know that they must select two additional points from the middle and towards the end of the text to support their response.

Please see an example of this plan in 2.6 on page 87.

2.4.2 Fishbone planning

The idea of the fishbone plan asks students to hang their ideas onto a thread where all ideas feed back into their initial argument (this is sometimes called their line of argument, thesis statement, or statement of purpose). For students who are able to write in a conceptual manner, the fishbone allows them to ensure that all of their ideas correspond with the original idea as they are literally planning by hanging ideas onto the central thread.

Much like the anchor plan, students can place these events in chronological order. It is a linear plan that enables them to see a clear process of formulating their response. We have had students who have drawn the plan across a whole page of A4 in an exam. In many ways, it is the visual that benefits them, as much as the positioning of their individual ideas.

Please see an example of this in 3.5 on page 114.

2.4.3 Grid/box planning

Planning within a grid enables students to match ideas across a paragraph or across texts. A positive with the grid planning is that students do not need to spend too long creating the boxes – we recommend encouraging them to do this freehand! Again, the grid offers a clearly defined number of ideas for students to plan, but will also encourage them to build on their initial ideas. We have seen, and used ourselves, plenty of versions of this planning style. A simple version might be the numbers 1-4 on the left-hand side, with an idea/quotation on the right. A more advanced might be idea on the left, with quotation, method, and other notes on the right. A colleague asks students to link each idea to their overall argument in each box, reinforcing the need to bring their ideas back to their main argument.

Grid planning is also ideal for comparison essays. A few simple tweaks make this style of planning suitable for the poetry comparison essay, for example. You might ask students to focus on two elements (for example, meaning and ideas, followed by structure and language) and then get them to use each. This structure encourages students to consider how they might make links between the two poems, whilst also providing them with a clear direction. We have seen students gain full marks (on the AQA specification) using this approach to poetry.

Please see an example of a single text box plan in 2.2 on page 65.

An example of a comparison box plan is in 4.1 on page 124.

2.4.4 Mind-map planning

The final planning format that is probably the most common, whilst arguably being the least effective, is using a mind-map/brainstorm/spider diagram (whatever name you use!) to map out the ideas the student has. The problem, of course, with using mind-maps as a planning structure is that we do not isolate their use to planning; students are encouraged to use them across subjects, and their purpose is often to generate ideas, rather than to structure them. Consider the following, taken from the AQA examiner's report for English Language Paper 1:

Occasionally, spider diagrams were used, which may generate ideas but do not help with organisation or cohesion [...] A lack of planning also resulted in unnecessarily lengthy responses, where the more a student wrote, the greater the deterioration in ideas, structure and accuracy.[2]

Whilst these comments were provided for the creative writing responses, the same can be said for the planning of literature responses, which also need cohesion – especially for the students aiming at the top of the mark scheme. That being said, we do still use this planning approach with some students. The key is to decide on a number of ideas (so that students do not simply add 15 random words around 'Lady Macbeth') and embed the practice that students then number their ideas (we often ask them to do this chronologically, but recognise that some teachers prefer going from extract to whole text, or ordering ideas from best to worst etc).

Please see an example of this in 1.1 on page 25.

3 Essay writing tips

3.1 Textual security

When engaging students in essay writing, the most important factor to consider is their understanding of the text itself. An essay is only as good as the student's knowledge of the text, and by this, we mean only their understanding of narrative: events and their chronology, characters and their idiosyncrasies, the themes and how they are developed. This is perhaps more so true of novels and plays, but there is also a need for students to fully understand the narratives that exist within poems. In an ideal world, students' knowledge of a text will become automatic, and it is with this automaticity that students will be able to perform excellent analysis and exploration of the texts in exam conditions.

There are many ways to build textual security, but fundamentally, it comes back to constant repetition and retrieval of the key elements of the narrative. Thankfully, an understanding of interleaving and spacing has ensured that curriculum maps now allow time to return to past texts, and a focus on retrieval practice means that knowledge has become embedded across a two-year course. It is crucial, that with the now closed book exams for English Literature, students enter the exam hall with a confident approach to the texts they study. Primarily we have ensured this through a rigorous and challenging approach to the knowledge expected of each text.

As explained in 2.1, our use of knowledge organisers function as the minimum expected understanding for our students. By the end of the course, students

---

2   (https://filestore.aqa.org.uk/sample-papers-and-mark-schemes/2017/june/AQA-87001-WRE-JUN17.PDF)

must move beyond a basic knowledge of the text to being able to recall key whole text methods, contextual factors, and flexible quotations. This textual security, where key components of the text become automatic to our student, frees up their cognitive space when writing. It is a vital, often overlooked, element of essay writing.

3.2 Building vocabulary and phrasing

It is now time to think of a particular type of student. Let's call them George. George is the first student in the class to put his hand up, appears to have excellent knowledge of the text and always answers correctly. All of his verbal responses point to him being a student who will perform well in an essay but, when George sits his assessments, it never matches what you expect of him. It leads to awkward parents' evening conversations where you say, 'George works really hard, he's got it all in his head, and he responds verbally, but he can't get it down on paper'. We've all taught a George.

The problem here, of course, is a discrepancy between spoken ability and written ability. It is also in what we expect of students when they respond in the classroom against what we demand of them in order to reach the top of the mark scheme in the literature GCSE. It's easy to hear George say:

> Macbeth starts off as a good guy, he fights for his country and is loyal to Duncan but by the end of the play, he doesn't care about Scotland and will kill anyone.

And feel pleased as a teacher that George understands the key narrative arc within the text. But, in an essay, we're expecting:

> Macbeth, at first appearing innately courageous and patriotic, later becomes a ruthless tyrant who makes murderous decisions recklessly and instinctively.

It's the same idea. There are plenty of ways to rewrite George's response with more nuanced vocabulary. It's these nuances that elevate student responses and allow them to tease out more developed ideas about texts. In every lesson, during every episode of a text, we should seek to expand and build on our students' vocabulary. Attaching phrases to particular characters, and then returning to them when moving on to a new text, will help to build a student's scheme around a particular world and enable them to advance their understanding. For example, considering why Scrooge is evidently avaricious and misanthropic in *A Christmas Carol* is crucial (these words do not have lower level examples that mean exactly the same thing – greedy and mean are not the same!) but how can you return to them when considering Mr Birling or Macbeth? After all, Macbeth is defined as avaricious by Malcolm in act 4, scene 3.

It is constantly returning to this vocabulary, expecting it to become part of students' understanding of the text, which will truly enhance their essay writing. Much like with textual security, once these words and phrases become automatic, students will begin to use them organically and fluently.

3.3 Conceptualised responses

When we begin to consider how students might move to a critical response, we turn to their ability to understand the text as a whole. This, for us, is a key indicator of a student's ability. A response that shows evidence of whole text understanding is most commonly considered a text with a line of argument – a response to a question, or focus, which can take an external view of the text. Another feature of these kinds of responses will be that the student understands that the text is a construct. Not once do they offer a comment on a character which makes them seem real; they recognise that characters are used as devices, by a writer, who is using the text as a vehicle.

This is actually pretty difficult to teach and for students to grasp. In reality, we see it as a threshold concept that must be passed in order for students to truly begin writing critical responses. It used to be defined in English teaching as 'flair' – we are not fans of 'flair'. Flair implies a natural, innate ability to respond to texts, but we fundamentally believe that conceptualised responses to texts can be taught. However, when they can be taught is a tricky consideration – we have both walked on this dangerous tightrope and taken a fall into the canyon below! In order for students to begin to develop conceptualised responses with an argument, they must already have absolute textual security and also be able to perform at a clear level consistently. These students will have hit a ceiling with a typically formed response – a simplified response that they might be achieving will be:

How does Priestley present the change in Sheila Birling?

Paragraph 1: Considers Sheila at the start and her attitude when getting the ring.

Paragraph 2: Discusses Sheila when she is interrogated and her remorse.

Paragraph 3: Explores how Sheila hands back the ring and what this represents.

Paragraph 4: Analyses Sheila following the inspector leaving and her changed actions.

Their response will hit all of the necessary elements of an essay, and be doing all the right things, but will often be limited to roughly two-thirds of the marks available. They might *seem* to understand that Sheila is not a real person, but at times, they lack full exploration of the implicit ideas within a text and have not got to grips with the writer's purpose. How do we move these students on?

This unspoken tightrope of English teaching – when is a class ready to be pushed a whole lot more – is a dangerous journey. If you try to teach conceptualised responses too soon, students will be confused and might even lose clarity, with responses being negatively affected rather than improved. Sometimes it's easy to tell when a class or individual student is ready to push to this top level – they start offering whole text approaches when faced with an essay question, rather than moving to isolated incidents. So being asked the question above, a student might say 'She is used as a symbol of hope, representing the journey the young upper class could take following World War 2' rather than an isolated response of 'Well, at the start, she is excitable and immature'.

One way to encourage conceptual responses is to offer open questions which consider the purpose of a text and ask all students to read out their ideas. You can then explain that each of these responses would be a line of argument to a narrower question and that each of these approaches will need different supporting evidence, analysis, and contextual understanding. An example I have used with *A Christmas Carol*:

> Teacher: What is the core message of *A Christmas Carol*, if you had to simplify it to a common saying or phrase?
>
> Student x: Money can't buy happiness
>
> Student y: Treat others as you would want to be treated
>
> Student z: It's never too late to change
>
> Teacher: Now, let's make this an exam question. You have the opening description of Scrooge, the one with all the lists and similes. Starting with this extract, how does Dickens present the transformation of Ebenezer Scrooge? You now need to come up with four moments in the text that all link together to your core statement, which proves that this is Dickens' overall message.

It's tasks like these that take students' essay writing away from looking at the micro, individual elements of texts and move to the macro, considering the text as a whole. The more exposure students get to tackling texts in this way and the more they are encouraged to begin the planning process with an overall idea/line of argument/statement of purpose/bigger picture/thesis statement (whatever you want to call it!) rather than moments in the text, the better their responses will inevitably become.

4 A curriculum approach to modelling

4.1 Compartmentalising the skills within English

Despite our love of worked examples, we are not suggesting that every student needs one in every unit we teach to every year group. Whilst model essays have their place at various stages of student learning, there is definitely a way to approach them across the five or potentially seven-year journey students will take in their learning of the discipline of English. If we see essay writing as a key component of succeeding in English, we must understand its constituent parts and ensure we teach them separately. Daisy Christodoulou's metaphor of a marathon works well here: a marathon runner does not train for a marathon by running marathons every day, so why do we train students for essay writing by asking them to write paragraphs when they arrive in Year 7?

Recent years in teaching have seen a change where overcomplicated tasks and activities have been stripped back to simple ideas executed really well. A renewed focus on curriculum has sought to ensure not only *how* we teach but also *what we teach* is interrogated appropriately. In English, this has predominantly focused on the content choices we make: concerns over the canon, decolonising the text choices, ensuring breadth and depth, and discussions over chronology. What this can often forget is the way we teach the skills of English – it is not uncommon for students to be taught a text in Year 7 and then be asked to write a paragraph on an element of that text. Our suggestion would be that to arrive at GCSE knowing how to write an essay is crucial, but we also have three years to get students ready to complete this monumental task. We need to create building blocks and separate the skills of essay writing. In doing so, we can embed skills properly, alongside a long-term approach to knowledge.

4.2 A long-term approach

Many schools have successfully made the move to a knowledge-rich curriculum which offers high value texts. As explained in 1.3, this is a situation we found ourselves in and it was a long and difficult journey. As this element of the curriculum is now embedded, we seek to continue reviewing how we can best support our students. As far as we see it, essay writing can be separated into the following core skills:

- Writing clear points which respond to a question/statement and offer an idea; making inferences beyond that idea.
- Selecting the best possible evidence as justification for an idea.
- Analysis skills, which can include analysis of language, structure, form, or any other choice made by the writer.

- Understanding of context, and the world that exists beyond the text, along with the writer's motivation.

It is undeniable that these skills are of a hierarchical nature. Without the ability to respond to a text to have an idea about it, students are unable to understand the world around the text or analyse the writer's methods. A long-term approach to essay writing would take this into account and seek to construct a curriculum where these skills are separated. Teachers should pay attention to those individual skills and understand all of their intricacies in order to deliver them across an entire term. As we return to the simplicity of knowledge retrieval, we must return to the simplicity of getting the basics of essay writing right first, before we overcomplicate it with acronyms and paragraphs, even essays, when students have only just arrived at secondary school.

4.3 Writing frames: giving and taking

Whilst there has been much discussion around the use of writing frames in English recently, the profession as a whole has not arrived at an agreed and satisfying conclusion. Many will still argue that writing frames have their place in all classrooms for all students, and some will argue that it is time to strip writing back to basics, giving students the freedom to write without any structure to follow. We contend that both of these binary approaches are dangerous. Without a doubt, there are some students who will need writing frames right up until their GCSEs, and we have seen success from students who have relied on writing frames (for example, students in literature gaining a grade 6, with a target of grade 3, who relied on paragraph structures to write their responses).

A suggested approach would be to build to a writing frame (whether an acronym, or the now popular what, how, why approach, first explained by Becky Wood) and then remove it. Once students have developed each of the individual skills an essay requires, perhaps across the first two years of Key Stage 3, they might then be exposed to a structure which enables them to merge these skills together. How this is delivered in the classroom is crucial: a paragraph structure is not dangerous in itself, but how it is presented to students and how it is utilised in lessons can be problematic. If students enter each lesson and are told 'we are writing a PETER paragraph today', the construction of the paragraph becomes an event by itself, rather than a cumulative performance and an amalgamation of a series of skills. Sometimes it is okay for students to not write a full paragraph – often, when they do, it is not actually what the teacher needs to achieve.

These are all questions and concerns we should have regarding teaching with paragraph structures and considering our long-term approach to essay writing. What this looks like in reality is actually quite complex. Below is an example framework (for Key Stage 3) that seeks to study texts in-depth, develop students' imaginative and viewpoint writing, as well as develop essay writing across three years. Alongside chosen texts, these are the specific skills students might look at to build into analytical responses.

5 So, how do I use this book?

This is the book we, as English teachers, need! We've tried to make it as user-friendly as possible so that you can use it in a variety of ways and gain both knowledge and hours from it.

You will find a selection of essays from the most commonly taught texts on the literature specification, *Macbeth*, *A Christmas Carol*, *An Inspector Calls*, and poems that are featured across different exam boards. Our core purpose in creating this book was to provide high level essays, essays for excellence, which would provide teachers with:

1. Exemplars to use with their classes.
2. Essays which could help improve subject knowledge.
3. A range of essays that could be used for standardising processes.

You will see that for each text, we have chosen one question and offered three answers to it. These answers are categorised as:

1. Critical: a high response which we consider to be the top of the mark scheme.
2. Thoughtful: a mid-high response that would sit just below 'critical' on the mark scheme.
3. Clear: a middle response that will be aspirational for students who are aiming to pass their English Literature GCSE. This sits below thoughtful.

We have designed each answer in order for them to be used with students in the classroom if needed. Each answer includes:

- Annotations (white box) explaining which skills the answer exemplifies.
- Questions (light grey box) that offer avenues to consider as a teacher or a student.
- A summary box (dark grey box) that explains why the answer is successful and why we have defined it as clear, thoughtful or critical.

Macbeth

Ideas about power

1.1 Starting with this extract, explore how Shakespeare presents ideas about power in *Macbeth*.

In the following extract from act 1 scene 3, Macbeth and Banquo are visited by Angus and Ross following the disappearance of the witches. Macbeth is given his new title of Thane of Cawdor.

ANGUS
We are sent
To give thee from our royal master thanks;
Only to herald thee into his sight,
Not pay thee.

ROSS
And, for an earnest of a greater honour,
He bade me, from him, call thee thane of Cawdor:
In which addition, hail, most worthy thane!
For it is thine.

BANQUO
What, can the devil speak true?

MACBETH
The thane of Cawdor lives: why do you dress me
In borrow'd robes?

ANGUS
Who was the thane lives yet;
But under heavy judgment bears that life
Which he deserves to lose. Whether he was combined
With those of Norway, or did line the rebel
With hidden help and vantage, or that with both
He labour'd in his country's wreck, I know not;
But treasons capital, confess'd and proved,
Have overthrown him.

MACBETH
[Aside] Glamis, and thane of Cawdor!
The greatest is behind.

1.1.1 Clear response

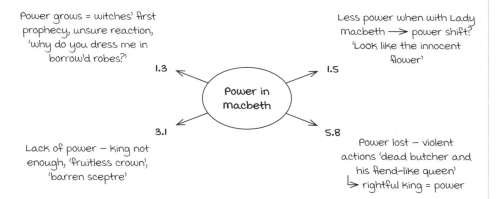

Power grows = witches' first prophecy, unsure reaction, 'why do you dress me in borrow'd robes?'

1.3

Less power when with Lady macbeth → power shift? 'Look like the innocent flower'

1.5

Power in macbeth

Lack of power – King not enough, 'fruitless crown', 'barren sceptre'

3.1

Power lost – violent actions 'dead butcher and his fiend-like queen' ⌐ rightful King = power

5.8

Power changes throughout *Macbeth,* from the people who have power, to how they get it, and what they do once they have it.

Early on in the play, Macbeth is given a new title and, with this new title, his mindset begins to change. It could be argued that his mindset has already changed with the prophecies he has received from the witches, but once given the title, he responds with 'why do you dress me in borrow'd robes?'. This question suggests Macbeth's confusion as he wonders not only what has happened to the former Thane of Cawdor, but also considers the prophecy he has just been given and, therefore, the power of the witches' prophecies. The 'robes' are a metaphor for Macbeth's power, suggesting he is not sure about the new clothing or power that he has been given as it seems to be 'borrow'd'. So, in this extract, Shakespeare establishes how power is something you can be given, like an item of clothing, but also encourages the audience to see this power as something that Macbeth has rightfully earned, as we know he is 'brave' and 'worthy' at the start of the play.

Interestingly, once Macbeth is shown with Lady Macbeth, we see a change in the power he appears to have. The power appears to shift onto her, and we notice that the power is not necessarily placed where we expect it to be. Her ability to persuade and manipulate Macbeth is evident throughout, but particularly when she tells him to 'look like the innocent flower but be the serpent under't'. Here, she attempts to control not only his physical appearance, but his behaviour too. The imperative verbs 'look' and 'be' highlight her power over Macbeth, as she feels able to command him without any repercussions. The juxtaposition between 'flower' and 'serpent' reveals her understanding of what they need to do to gain power and it is, therefore, Lady Macbeth who controls the situation and their rise to power and ensures they gain it later on in the play. Perhaps Shakespeare is highlighting the dangers of a woman going outside of her role. In Jacobean England, a woman should follow the decision making of the man,

How could this introduction be improved?

There is clear explanation of the writer's methods here, with some valid comments made about the various effects of these choices.

Why might the candidate have chosen to write their response in chronological order?

This quotation choice supports the discussion over how power changes throughout the play.

How could this comment on context be more detailed or specific to the play?

Specific quotations are used here to illustrate the point that is made; they allow clear focus on the task given.

How could the candidate ensure this part of their response does not become too narrative?

Good understanding of the relationship between the text and its context.

Could the candidate make comments about Lady Macbeth here too? What could they say about this quotation?

Has this message been clear throughout the whole response?

so both characters going against this causes a spiral of chaos from which the country cannot escape.

Once Macbeth has gained the power he wanted, it seems that it is never enough for him to be satisfied. Now king, he begins to question how much power he truly has, with the soliloquy in the first scene of act 3 having him consider the power he now holds, and deciding he has a 'fruitless crown' on his head and a 'barren sceptre' in his grip. These oxymorons present us with a contradiction: Macbeth has some power, with the 'crown' and 'sceptre', but he sees this as an empty power. We can infer that the power seems empty to him because, despite being king, he knows that his power has an end, as he heard the prophecy of Banquo from the witches that his children will be king and Macbeth's power is not enough until he ensures that Banquo and Fleance are dead. As Macbeth's power grows, so does his hunger for complete power, and it is when he realises that his crown is 'fruitless' that he commits the murder of his once best friend Banquo. Shakespeare is warning the audience here: power in the wrong hands will never be enough and that getting power in the wrong way (in this case through regicide, perhaps the link to the Gunpowder plot of 1605 and the failed attempt of regicide) will lead to the downfall of not only the person committing treason but anyone in their path, and the country as a whole.

In the final scene of the play, we realise that power is fragile and can easily be taken away. Both Macbeth and Lady Macbeth end the play as victims of their power, as they are absent and are viewed by other people, therefore their power is completely removed, and they are now simply known as a 'dead butcher and his fiend-like queen'. The metaphor of Macbeth as a 'butcher', rather than calling him a monarch, now takes away all of his power. He now simply represents a violent 'butcher' who commits regular murders of innocent animals, rather than any title with status and power. With Malcolm saying this, we are reminded that the power is now back with the rightful king. This is Shakespeare's message to the audience: ultimately only certain people (those chosen by God) have any right to power, especially the total power that a king has.

Clear response
This answer successfully offers clear ideas about the theme of power and tracks the change in power throughout the play. The four separate ideas show strong knowledge of the play and how the theme is used by Shakespeare however, the response seems to offer very isolated ideas and each the candidate would benefit from thinking of a more specific overview and building a more cohesive argument throughout. The analysis is clear throughout, and the relationship of the context to the text is considered regularly.

1.1.2 Thoughtful response

Throughout *Macbeth*, the power shifts and changes, and eventually it corrupts those who do not deserve it. Macbeth and Lady Macbeth's hunger for power is what ultimately leads to their downfall, as both of them struggle with the power they so desperately desire. Shakespeare reinforces the destructive impact of power to his audience, a clear warning against any treasonous thoughts against the reigning monarch, King James.

Macbeth's power grows within the first scene we encounter him, as with the title of Thane of Cawdor, his struggle to understand his power begins. When given the title, Macbeth's first response is 'Why do you dress me in borrow'd robes?' – a clear indication of his uncertainty around the power he has been given. The question, almost rhetorical, appears ambiguous: Angus answers with details of the Thane of Cawdor's disloyalty but ignores the suggestion that the title is 'borrow'd'. This metaphorical reference to 'borrow'd robes' indicates that Macbeth sees power as something that can be passed on, like an item of clothing – but also foreshadows the idea that it can be removed if the clothing does not fit, as happens to Macbeth with his execution at the end of the play. We can also suggest that the clothing, or power given, is corrupted. The fact the robes are 'borrow'd' from the former Thane of Cawdor, who we shortly learn from Angus has committed an act of 'treason' – so Macbeth being handed this title also foreshadows the treasonous act he will later commit. Shakespeare is immediately warning the audience of how power is not an easy thing to deal with once you have it – perhaps Macbeth is right to be wary of these 'borrow'd robes' as the prophecy being fulfilled is his first step on his destructive journey.

Power is presented as a much more complex entity once we encounter Lady Macbeth and her powerful influence over Macbeth. Lady Macbeth's hunger for power, fuelling Macbeth's earlier signs of 'black and deep desires', is shown not only in her soliloquies, but also in her interaction with Macbeth, as she tells him to 'Look like the innocent flower but be the serpent under't'. Shakespeare shifts the power to Lady Macbeth, and the 'brave' and 'noble' character from earlier in the play is reduced to a puppet who can be commanded. Notably, the imperative verbs used here (both 'look' and 'be') begin a pattern of imperative verbs used by Lady Macbeth right up until the power corrupts her sanity. During the regicide committed in act 2, scene 2 she again tells Macbeth to 'give' and 'go', and these imperative verbs are used by Shakespeare to repeatedly highlight that the power lies with Lady Macbeth, at least initially, in their marriage. It does not take long for this to shift following their coronation and this, again, reminds us of the struggles of power once it is obtained. Shakespeare warns against all people going against their societal role. Macbeth should remain a thane unless God chooses him as king, but also, Lady Macbeth subverts the gender norms of Jacobean England and in doing so forces power upon her marriage that ultimately neither her or her husband can withstand.

> This is a thoughtful opening where there seems to be a conceptual approach to the question.

> **Consider the terminology used here – how has the candidate used it to comment on the theme of power?**

> The interpretation is well-developed and shows a thorough understanding of the whole text, beyond the extract given.

> **How are quotations embedded here to support the ideas given about power?**

> The examination of methods becomes thoughtful when the use of imperative verbs is considered across the play, an interesting consideration of methods throughout.

How could these comments about fertility be linked to attitudes towards the monarchy in Jacobean England?

Strong and secure understanding of the text shown at this point as the idea is extended beyond the moment given.

Macbeth's struggle with power, once it is gained, is evident in his increasing distrust both of his own authority and Banquo's prophecy. His realisation that he wears a 'fruitless crown' and holds a 'barren sceptre' is indicative of his growing realisation that no matter what power he obtains, it will never fully be enough. For him his power is 'fruitless' and 'barren', with this natural imagery holding connotations of infertility; essentially, Macbeth is reminding himself that without an heir, his 'crown' is 'fruitless'. Arguably, these oxymorons are symbolic of the conflicted emotions Macbeth feels regarding his power: he has it, so he should feel like a king with a crown, but due to Banquo's prophecy, his power is not absolute. This manifests itself as fear, as Macbeth mentions within this soliloquy 'our fears in Banquo', and this ultimately leads to Banquo's murder. It is in this moment that the power shifts between Macbeth and Lady Macbeth, as he decides not to confide in her, only telling her to 'be innocent of the knowledge'. This shift in power is indicated in the shift in use of imperative verbs, and Macbeth begins to struggle with his power, and struggle to maintain it, and this leads to mindless murders in order to feel secure as king. As Macbeth's power grows, so does his uncertainty surrounding it, and Shakespeare warns his audience of the chaos that ensues when power consumes us and our humanity is removed.

Using single word quotations allows the candidate to quickly cover multiple ideas about power in a succinct way.

Macbeth's struggle for power, and his struggle with it, ultimately leads to his downfall, where he is stripped of all status and nobility. This once 'noble' character who was offered an additional title for his 'worthy' actions, is now reduced to nothing, merely a 'dead butcher'. Earlier repeated references to Macbeth as a 'tyrant' at least afforded him some power and status, but now he is simply a 'butcher', given no authority but over the carcass of animals. This metaphor spotlights the violence of Macbeth, rather than the power he once held, and so in death, he loses the very thing he fought for. Shakespeare here reinforces the Jacobean belief in the Divine Right, reasserting that Macbeth's reign was always 'fruitless' because he was not the chosen monarch, a potentially topical reference to the execution of Guy Fawkes, an event that took place within the year of Macbeth's first performance to King James. And one with a similar ending: those who seek and struggle with power that is not theirs will ultimately be punished.

How is this historical moment used to support the candidate's comments about power?

Thoughtful response
This response is particularly strong within the AO2 elements of the mark scheme. We see considerable examination of methods, in particular the moment where imperative verbs are tracked across the play is particularly thoughtful. There is some clever integrated use of references to support ideas about power. In order to improve this response, the ideas could follow a single line of argument about power.

1.1.3 Critical response

Constantly fluctuating and ultimately being placed with its rightful owner, the fragility of power is a central theme in *Macbeth* and one which dictates relationship dynamics and the development of Macbeth as a character. Through Macbeth's gain but then loss of power, Shakespeare warns his audience of the fatal danger of pursuing power which is not rightfully yours, and warns them of the consequences, obviously appeasing to and reassuring King James, despite his fragile reign of power.

> This is already a critical consideration of the theme in the question, with a line of argument established.

Significantly, the fragile nature of power is established immediately, and Macbeth's awareness of this is evident from as early as act 1, scene 3. When given the title of Thane of Cawdor, Macbeth asks 'why do you dress me in borrow'd robes?' Here, Shakespeare places Macbeth in a difficult position, as he is given a title he believes someone currently holds, but the comment offers far more complex implications. Macbeth's reluctance with this immediate question indicates his awareness of the instability of power – how it cannot be held by more than one person – and is indicative of his later consideration that Malcolm is a 'step' which 'lies' in his 'way'. The motif of clothing is used throughout *Macbeth* and can be aligned with status, and at this moment begins the sense that Macbeth's status never quite fits him. Banquo later in this scene calls the new title 'strange garments', but both of these are spoken in Macbeth's presence, so the ill-fitting clothing is something he is aware of. The fragile nature of his power is further highlighted within the motif in act 5, where even minor characters comment on how Macbeth's status does not fit: 'now does he feel his title hang loose [...] like a giant's robe upon a dwarfish thief'. Shakespeare moves from something being 'borrow'd' or 'strange' to hanging totally loose; the juxtaposition of 'giant' and 'dwarfish' being indicative of how unsuitable Macbeth is to reign over Scotland, with the hyperbolic simile overall conveying the absurdity of Macbeth being king of Scotland. This motif establishes how power is fragile and complex, and Shakespeare makes the power being given to Malcolm a far more agreeable moment, hinting that the 'robe' of a king can only be worn by the one with the divine right to rule.

> **How does this opening sentence support the ideas given in the introduction?**

> Consideration of a whole text method, like a motif, is often an indicator of a high level response. Here it shows convincing and thorough knowledge of the whole play.

Manipulative and destructive, yet ultimately fragile herself, Lady Macbeth's role within the power dynamics of the play cannot be ignored. She deftly orchestrates an undetected regicide without getting her own hands dirty (initially, at least) and she becomes a puppet master to her own husband, a man recently heralded as 'worthy' of the king's favour and titles, but now reduced to a submissive man who is told by his wife how to behave, to 'look like the innocent flower and be the serpent under't'. This deceptive behaviour seeps from Lady Macbeth to Macbeth, with the suggested biblical allusion to Genesis through the 'serpent' hinting at the dark temptations which Lady Macbeth offers to her husband. However, the power within this relationship is undoubtedly fragile,

> **How does this idea, despite being about a new character, tie into the overall response to the text?**

The candidate critically considers the use of imperative verbs here and how they are utilised in more than one moment in the text.

How are quotations used here to show excellent knowledge of the whole play?

The candidate clearly understands how power is fragile and this overview given at the start is continued throughout each paragraph, ensuring an argument is developed in detail and proven throughout.

The response is mature and perceptive, as the candidate begins to pull together the threads of their argument about fragile power and link it to the ending.

as whilst we might consider Lady Macbeth as the dominant figure here, this balance tips later on in the play, as early as act 3. With the murder of Banquo Macbeth cuts his puppet strings, and he grapples the power away from Lady Macbeth, who he tells to 'be innocent of the knowledge'. His phrasing here lies parallel to Lady Macbeth's from act 1, scene 5: both use the imperative verb 'be' to force a certain behaviour from their partner, and both ironically define their spouse's actions to be 'innocent', which neither are considered by the end of the play. Innocence and guilt would surely call forth to King James's mind his own dealings with those who threaten his throne and their deceptively 'innocent' behaviour. As *Macbeth* was initially written for the court, we can see Shakespeare unpacking the deceit at the heart of the unstable power both within the play and within Jacobean England.

Despite gaining the total power of ruling Scotland, Macbeth's unease around his power continues once he is placed on the throne. This is most evident in his soliloquy in act 3, scene 1, where he rightfully raises his 'fears in Banquo' (this soliloquy follows Banquo's own soliloquy and his 'fear' of Macbeth's 'foul' play) and his growing concern of his 'fruitless crown' and 'barren sceptre'. Evidently, Macbeth's unease is fully realised as the play progresses, with Fleance's escape meaning Banquo's prophecy remains accurate, and with his power proving 'fruitless' as it only leads to his own demise. The 'barren' nature of his power is inextricably linked to the infertility of the Macbeth's marriage, where a lack of child means a lack of heir, and it is this that means their power is fundamentally temporary. The use of 'crown' and 'sceptre' within his soliloquy is interesting; these inanimate objects that are representative of power and status are empty to Macbeth, but within the public sphere mean he actually holds absolute power. Of course, he is later defined as 'bloody-sceptred' by Macduff, an explicit link to the motif of blood as guilt, where Macbeth's heinous acts are visible on the very objects that should indicate his power. From this Shakespeare reminds us that power in itself is not only fragile but something that is both given and taken away. Arguably, Macbeth is never powerful, he just has it, but he never truly understands what he does have until he forces himself into a state of losing it.

At the close of the play, Macbeth's power is no longer fragile; it is non-existent, and his own endless cycle of chaos and destruction is what removes all power from him. Despite acknowledging early on that 'blood will have blood', Macbeth never realises that his actions will eventually lead to his own blood being spilt, or if he does realise it at this point, he does nothing to prevent it. The power Macbeth has as King of Scotland is never enough, because power by its very nature is fragile, and we see this through his mindless actions which only lead to his downfall: the murder of Banquo, returning to the witches, killing Macduff's family, and then believing he is invincible and can withstand an army of 10,000 men. Shakespeare has no choice but to end the play with Macbeth's death and Malcolm reinstated as the rightful king of Scotland. In order for the play to be performed beyond the confines of the court, Shakespeare has to offer a brutal punishment to Macbeth, and ensure Malcolm (who at times is arguably presented as ineffective) and his reinstatement as Scotland's ruler is one that is celebrated alongside Macbeth's death. Allowing Malcolm the final words of the play, with Macbeth only being called a 'dead butcher', Macbeth is eventually stripped of the fragile power he so desperately craved. He is metaphorically no longer a 'king' or 'tyrant', but a lowly 'butcher' – a title stripped of all dignity and status. It is in this moment that Shakespeare's final warning comes to fruition: any fragile power gained is irrelevant, it is how you are remembered that counts – even Macbeth's name is not spoken, a clear indication of where all power lies, with the soon to be 'crowned' King Malcolm.

> **How do the links between text and context become integrated into the response here?**
>
> The use of single word references serve to support the interpretation and conclusion reached.

Critical response

This response offers a well-developed argument that is centred around the notion that power is presented as fragile. This idea is then convincingly developed throughout, with analysis and contextual comments used to support this overall idea. There are judicious references embedded throughout the response, used well to develop this personal approach to the question. The analysis is fine-grained and precise, considering whole text choices as well as analysis at a more granular level. Finally, the candidate knows the text extremely well.

The influence of the witches

1.2 Starting with this extract, explore how Shakespeare presents the influence of the witches in *Macbeth*.

In the following extract from act 4, scene 1, Macbeth has returned to the witches. The witches anticipate his arrival.

Second Witch
By the pricking of my thumbs,
Something wicked this way comes.
Open, locks,
Whoever knocks!

Enter MACBETH

MACBETH
How now, you secret, black, and midnight hags!
What is't you do?

ALL
A deed without a name.

MACBETH
I conjure you, by that which you profess,
Howe'er you come to know it, answer me:
Though you untie the winds and let them fight
Against the churches; though the yesty waves
Confound and swallow navigation up;
Though bladed corn be lodged and trees blown down;
Though castles topple on their warders' heads;
Though palaces and pyramids do slope
Their heads to their foundations; though the treasure
Of nature's germens tumble all together,
Even till destruction sicken; answer me
To what I ask you.

First Witch
Speak.

Second Witch
Demand.

Third Witch
We'll answer.

First Witch

Say, if thou'dst rather hear it from our mouths,

Or from our masters?

MACBETH

Call 'em; let me see 'em.

1.2.1 Clear response

I.I – When shall we three meet again In thunder, lightning, or in rain? **Second Witch** When the hurlyburly's done, When the battle's lost and won. **Third Witch** – there to meet with Macbeth
I.III – 'Stay you imperfect speakers, tell me more' Speak, if you can: what are you? 'he seems rapt withal' 'have we eaten on the insane root that takes the reason prisoner?' 'Your children shall be kings'; 'you shall be king' 'Can the devil speak true?'
I.V 'Come you spirits that tend on mortal thoughts, unsex me here'
IV.I 'by the pricking of my thumbs something wicked this way comes' 'Secret, black and midnight hags' 'I conjure you' 'Answer me to what I ask you'

Macbeth opens with the witches on the heath. The witches already seem to know that Macbeth will come to them as the they say that they are 'there to meet with Macbeth'. Shakespeare here shows the power of the witches as they can see the future and accurately predict what will happen as the play develops. Shakespeare uses pathetic fallacy in the opening of the play as the witches explain that they shall meet in 'thunder, lightning or in rain', setting the tone as stormy, showing that the witches know that there will be unrest. The witches and their words are important to the play as a whole because Shakespeare deliberately chooses to use them as the first characters who speak to introduce what will happen.

Macbeth and Banquo first meet the witches in act 1, scene 3 and Macbeth commands the witches to 'speak if you can: what are you?' This shows that

The candidate here opens by explaining the significance of the witches. They show an understanding of why the witches are used by Shakespeare and the effect they may have on the play.

The candidate begins their response by focusing on Macbeth's first interaction with the witches instead of the extract. Why might this be a successful approach for the candidate?

References to the context support the candidate's understanding of main ideas.

Macbeth is unsure as to who the witches are, but he still speaks to them, showing his curious nature. He uses an imperative verb to show that he tries to order them about. This would not surprise an audience as men, such as Macbeth, would have had more natural authority over women in the patriarchal society. As the witches attempt to depart, Macbeth commands them to 'stay, you imperfect speakers' so that they can 'tell [him] more'. This suggests that he thinks he can control them and also that he wants to believe in what they have told him. This shows the influence that the witches have over Macbeth as he is almost desperate for them to stay again as he tries to order them about using imperatives once again. Banquo does try to speak to the witches, but he is not as demanding as Macbeth and he recognises the influence that the witches are having almost immediately on Macbeth as he comments that Macbeth is 'rapt withal'. This magical language shows that Macbeth is almost under the witches' spell after his first meeting with them.

The candidate selects some relevant detail, but what could they do with this to improve their response?

The response is largely descriptive here, yet the candidate considers the influence that the witches have on other characters in the play to try to develop their ideas.

When the witches have left, Macbeth seems to be excited by their prophecies and tells Banquo that his 'children shall be kings' in order for Banquo to reassure him that he 'shall be king'. Banquo is more suspicious of the witches than Macbeth however, when Macbeth is made the Thane of Cawdor, Banquo questions, 'what can the devil speak true?' suggesting that he believes the witches are a negative influence with evil powers similar to the devil.

The influence of witches and spirits are felt throughout the play and Lady Macbeth actually calls to them in act 1, scene 5. She says 'come you spirits who tend on mortal thoughts, unsex me here' and we can see that she uses imperative language just like Macbeth did earlier to try to command them to do things. Lady Macbeth is different to Macbeth here though as it appears that she understands the power that they have as she believes that they actually have the ability to 'unsex' her. This would be a difficult thing to do so she must understand the influence and abilities that the spirits and witches have.

The candidate links the presentation of the witches at the start to the end of the play here, which allows them to comment on the structure of the play. This helps the candidate to draw their ideas together and show how the influence has changed across the course of the play.

Towards the end of the play, Macbeth's attitude changes towards the witches but he still understands and shows the audience the important influence that he believes them to have over his life. Macbeth calls them 'secret, black and midnight hags' which links to the start of the play with the darkness of the storm and 'midnight'. This time, however, he knows them to be 'hags' which would have been associated at the time with old women who would have been suspected to be witches; an image that an audience at the time would have been wary of. Instead of avoiding them though, we see the influence that they have over Macbeth as he actively approaches them and tries to control them. This would have left an audience aware of the negative influence that they were having on Macbeth, which is even more clearly shown when he says 'I conjure you' to them. This use of the magical verb 'conjure' shows that he is trying to be like the witches and enchant them into doing something for him instead of him ordering them to do things like he did at the beginning of the play. This clearly shows the influence that the witches had on men like Macbeth and society at the time as he not only relies on them for information but actively begins to speak using their style of language.

Clear response

This response is successful at this level as the candidate is able to explain the influence that the witches have over characters within the play, and they are also able to show how this influence changes as the play develops. There are many stand-alone ideas within this response that show the influence of the witches at different points. In order to progress to the next level, the candidate would benefit from taking a more joined up approach and considering the overall influence the witches had. There are attempts to comment on language and method use within this response to highlight ideas and the audience and context are also referred to.

1.2.2 Thoughtful response

Mysterious, powerful and unrivalled in their influence upon Macbeth, Shakespeare's witches are often seen to be the key to Macbeth's unravelling within the play. Through Shakespeare's choice to open with the figures of the witches there is the suggestion that these three 'women' are a governing influence over the tumultuous tragedy that unfolds within the play.

> This thoughtful yet snappy opening sets out the candidate's views in response to the question.

The opening scene of the play positions the witches at the eye of the storm both metaphorically and physically. The opening line indeed shows the witches questioning 'when shall we three meet again in thunder, lightning or in rain?' Shakespeare's use of pathetic fallacy here reveals to a contemporaneous reader the associations with darkness and evil that primarily need to be made. The weather itself sets the scene for disturbances within the atmosphere that can foreshadow to an audience the turbulent weather pattern that will ultimately play out within the human world. Almost immediately following this, the third witch asserts that the 'posters of the sea and land' are 'there to meet with Macbeth' which, right from the very opening of the play, links the witches to the eponymous character. This is a tie that appears to be indissoluble as the play develops and, in fact, only strengthens further.

> The candidate develops their ideas in response to the question by posing increasingly thoughtful suggestions about the impact that specific methods have on an audience's understanding.

An audience first sees Macbeth on stage with the witches in act 1, scene 3 – a mere scene between them prophetically announcing that they will do just so. This does two things for an audience. Firstly, it acknowledges the 'more [...] than mortal thoughts' that the witches possess, and it also shows the complex relationship that Macbeth embarks upon with the witches as they exert such a strong influence upon his course. Whilst Banquo and Macbeth are greeted by the witches together, perhaps surprisingly, it is Banquo who first engages with them. This allows for Macbeth to take an initial step back to almost process what to say to them and also decide what he wants from them. Macbeth's first address

> **The candidate here touches upon the impact the witches have on Banquo. How could the candidate develop this idea further to ensure that their point is made clear on why it is interesting that Banquo first engages with them?**

to the witches conveys his perceived dominance over them as he instructs them to 'speak, if you can: what are you?' Primarily, the imperative verb reveals his desire to engage with them, yet more subtly the conditional conjunction 'if' suggests, at this point, that he is unsure of their abilities. It is this tentative curiosity that allows the influence of the witches to go somewhat unrecognised by Macbeth until much later within the play when he exposes just how much he comes to rely on them and their words.

Whilst Macbeth appears to be 'rapt' entirely by the prophecies that follow, their potentially negative influence is highlighted to the careful audience member by Banquo who, once Macbeth is made the Thane of Cawdor, asks 'can the devil speak true?' This damning address term used by Banquo to describe the witches could signify his ability to see what Macbeth cannot: the witches are to be categorised in the same way as the devil. This, therefore, highlights to an audience, especially of the Jacobean era, that these witches were to be avoided and would only result in evil and damnation.

Fascination with witchcraft is woven throughout the play by Shakespeare in his effort to garner the favour of King James I, yet in addition to this, an audience is also treated to the presentation of the patriarchal society at work. Lady Macbeth is linked to ideas of witchcraft, which shows the treatment of both women and witches in an insightful way. Whilst Macbeth calls directly to the witches who are seen to engage him in conversation, Lady Macbeth is seen to go one step further and attempts to 'conjure' them herself. This allows for Shakespeare to show the danger of women who fraternise with witchcraft and later warns of their fateful ending. Lady Macbeth implores the 'spirits who tend on mortal thoughts' to 'unsex [her] here'. She commands them to 'come' to her using the same imperative language as utilised by her husband in the earlier scenes. Not only does this show that Lady Macbeth requires the help of others to de-feminise herself should she wish to hold any real power, but it also highlights the unacknowledged influence that the witches and spirits of the supernatural world can exert on the living, 'mortal' world.

Within act 4, scene 1, we see Macbeth return to the witches after attempting to reassure himself that they are the ones who can influence and advise him of his fate. Whilst Macbeth clearly believes that he is meeting on his own terms, this is absolutely not the case; he yet again underestimates the influence that they continue to lord over him. Not only are the witches preoccupied with evil, but they are also preoccupied with him who, in turn, becomes an evil figure within the play which, some may argue, is all down to the influence of the witches. Gone is Macbeth's curiosity surrounding the witches, his quizzical questions instead modulated into statements such as 'how now, you secret, black and midnight hags'. Shakespeare's use of the semantic field of darkness here serves to remind us of the 'black and deep' influences, which the witches have projected onto

---

Here, the candidate begins to build upon their original ideas and ensures that they also address the context of the play.

How has the candidate successfully woven their contextual understanding with their knowledge of the text to support their argument here?

The candidate builds on ideas within this paragraph showing their ability to manage multiple sources of evidence to support an overall argument.

Structurally, this response returns to ideas that have been previously expressed and examined. The candidate explains the relevance of these connections.

What does the use of single word quotations do to the ending of this response?

Macbeth throughout the play that have led to his 'scorpion' filled mind that he cannot ever escape.

> **Thoughtful response**
> This response shows that the candidate is able to form a cohesive argument by referring to multiple points across the play that all link together to support the candidate's overarching idea about the influence of the witches. The writing is fluent; the candidate presents their ideas in a developed and thoughtful way. The candidate shows an increasingly thoughtful appreciation of how meanings and ideas are shaped through language and structure that is supported through careful selection of detail with terminology used accurately throughout. It is clear that this candidate knows much more about the text than they have written about, which is evidenced through their confident use of drop quotations throughout their response.

1.2.3 Critical response

With an unparalleled influence over the action within Shakespeare's Scottish play, the 'weird sisters' are undoubtedly the key to much of the tragic upset that is experienced both by the eponymous character and those of the Jacobean society of the play in which they exist. Notably, the witches, as they are commonly referred to by a modern audience, are not actually denoted as such within the play text at any point. Moreover, they are directly named the 'weird sisters' or the 'weyward sisters', with the latter term suggesting the ways in which the witches are seen to transgress the social norms of the society they live in. The adjective 'weyward' suggests that these figures are potentially difficult to control or whose actions are difficult to predict as a result of their wilful or perverse behaviour. This acknowledgement could, therefore, also suggest that these characters are inextricably bound with authority and the political dealings of the society, rather than just being viewed as magical 'spirits' who have the ability to influence Macbeth's fate.

> The candidate's opening view is presented persuasively and assuredly. This view is supported by some intricate analysis right from the very beginning which focuses on an idea which is perhaps not an obvious reading of the text.

Shakespeare, in an effort to appease the views of King James I, may use the characters of the 'weird sisters' to highlight the dangerous actions of women who believe themselves to be more powerful than society allows for them to be. This is clearly seen within the opening scene where the third witch acknowledges that they are 'there to meet with Macbeth'. Whilst this may ostensibly be suggestive of their supernatural powers, it is also a comment on the power and influence that they believe themselves to have. This leads us to question whether the witches' prophecies are more than just a self-fulfilling prophecy. We must wonder whether they in fact know that Macbeth will become king (which shows the belief in their own self-importance as they engage with the future monarch), or whether they merely shape the future for Macbeth as a result of their words instead of necessarily being able to foresee the future that will unravel.

> **How does the candidate use tentative language here to pose suggestions about interpretations? Why might this be a successful approach?**

The candidate
engages with multiple
interpretations cogently
here. This shows real
engagement with the text
through careful textual
analysis.

**How does the candidate
weave in their analysis
with an understanding
of the text? How does
this support their overall
argument successfully?**

The candidate returns to
their argument posed in
the opening. This keeps a
cohesive and consistent
thread running.

The candidate suggests
their own interpretation
of the question here. This
shows their ability to
consistently handle the text
with confidence.

**How does the candidate
strengthen their
argument here regarding
the influence of the
witches?**

Meeting for the first time, physically, on the heath in act 1, scene 3, it is Banquo that takes the lead in discourse with the 'inhabitants [...] who should be women'. This allows for Shakespeare to create space between the witches and Macbeth initially that he is then quick to fill and dominate. Commanding the witches to 'Speak, if you can', Macbeth asserts the position that his gender affords him. He uses this initial imperative verb with ease before continuing to order them twice more to 'stay' and 'speak' for a second time. A confident reader of the text may recognise that whilst Macbeth appears to be in control of the witches through the way in which he speaks to them, this is not entirely the case. Moreover, the witches exert a paramount influence over him without him even realising as they do not 'stay' and they also leave him with an insatiable appetite to learn more which Banquo acknowledges as him being 'rapt withal'. Macbeth is, even at this early point in the play, consumed by the witches' influence to the point where even his closest friend questions whether they have indeed 'eaten on the insane root', a reference that does not fail to 'conjure' up ideas of potions and concoctions of the supernatural's production in the audience's mind. It is, however, at this point that we must examine the true influence the witches do indeed have. Banquo appears to see them for what they are, corresponding with the view King James would have undoubtedly wanted his audiences to have – witches are products of the 'devil' and no good will come of them. Banquo is not influenced by them in the same way that Macbeth appears to be. Banquo hears the prophecy promised to himself, 'your children shall be kings', yet he does not act on these words. This could, therefore, suggest a possible alternative to the path that Macbeth chooses to tread, but it also allows us to understand that Macbeth is susceptible to the influence of such otherworldly beings.

As opposed to purely considering the influence that the witches have, it may be worthwhile considering how easily Macbeth can be influenced by those who he believes have his best interests at heart. His wife, Lady Macbeth herself has been linked to having supernatural ties by critics throughout history and we, as readers, are aware of the influence that she too has on her husband. Notably, in act 3, scene 5, Lady Macbeth implores the 'spirits who tend on mortal thoughts' to 'unsex [me] here' where she is seen to privately appeal to the 'spirits' for help. Not only does this allow us to question the nature of Lady Macbeth, but it also allows Shakespeare to gain favour with his king as he subtly warns of the dangers of such a relationship when we witness the 'cry of women within' much later in the play as she meets her own untimely death. Not only does Lady Macbeth seek the help of the 'spirits', but she too acknowledges the influence that they could have on her future. The limitations of her gender are recognised by her as she appeals for them to 'unsex' her, thus removing from her all that makes her female and that could, therefore, hinder her potential as the country's queen. This is an insurmountable amount of influence and power that she attributes to these 'spirits' in a similar fashion to the trust and faith that her husband places in the 'weird sisters'.

As the second meeting between Macbeth and the witches comes to fruition in act 4, scene 1, it is clear that Macbeth believes that this is an encounter of his own orchestration. Macbeth makes it clear to his wife that he 'will, to the weird sisters: More shall they speak' where, in actual fact, the witches are ready to welcome him back into their realm with their ominous assertion that 'by the pricking of my thumbs, something wicked this way comes'. Not only can the witches sense that Macbeth's arrival is imminent, but they also strip him of his humanity and instead opt to refer to him as 'something'. This final meeting between the 'weird sisters' and Macbeth brings us back to the tempestuous atmosphere witnessed at the opening of the play with the thunder, lightning and rain. The metaphorical and physical storm is now replaced by intolerable darkness present in Shakespeare's choice of semantic field. Gone are the 'inhabitants of the earth' and in their place are the 'secret, black and midnight hags'. Not only does Shakespeare reinforce to an audience the inescapable abyss into which Macbeth has embarked, but he also keenly reminds us of the dangers of not recognising the dangerous influence that others exert on you both consciously and subconsciously.

Notice how the candidate writes in a fluent way that develops their critical style here.

To the very end, the candidate continues to focus on micro elements that enhance their understanding of the macro. The argument is tied up neatly and successfully.

Critical response

This is an assured, personal response from the candidate that demonstrates a high level of engagement with the text. References are seamlessly woven into the analysis throughout and are commented on with precision and accuracy. The candidate offers tentative judgements throughout the response as they suggest multiple layers of meaning with the play. The response provides convincing explorations of several ideas that support the candidate's argument and show their ability to move between the general and specific with ease.

Macbeth as a tragic hero

1.3 Starting with this extract, explore how far Shakespeare presents Macbeth as a tragic hero.

In the following extract from act 3, scene 1, Macbeth is considering his relationship with Banquo and his new status as the King of Scotland.

> MACBETH
> To be thus is nothing;
> But to be safely thus. Our fears in Banquo
> Stick deep; and in his royalty of nature
> Reigns that which would be fear'd: 'tis much he dares;
> And, to that dauntless temper of his mind,
> He hath a wisdom that doth guide his valour
> To act in safety. There is none but he
> Whose being I do fear: and, under him,
> My Genius is rebuked; as, it is said,
> Mark Antony's was by Caesar. He chid the sisters
> When first they put the name of king upon me,
> And bade them speak to him: then prophet-like
> They hail'd him father to a line of kings:
> Upon my head they placed a fruitless crown,
> And put a barren sceptre in my gripe,
> Thence to be wrench'd with an unlineal hand,
> No son of mine succeeding. If 't be so,
> For Banquo's issue have I filed my mind;
> For them the gracious Duncan have I murder'd;
> Put rancours in the vessel of my peace
> Only for them; and mine eternal jewel
> Given to the common enemy of man,
> To make them kings, the seed of Banquo kings!
> Rather than so, come fate into the list.
> And champion me to the utterance! Who's there!

1.3.1 Critical response

Imbued with a sense of heroism in that Macbeth is praised by his king at the opening of the play for his contribution to his country's 'valiant' efforts against the Norwegian army, Macbeth can be seen at the beginning of the play as a character who many would look up to and respect. He is seen to, along with Banquo, fight bravely for the king's honour and supports Scotland in returning as victorious. For this loyalty and strength in battle he is revered by his peers

The candidate identifies how Macbeth is presented in the opening of the play. This is well supported by an explanation of the text alongside an awareness of Shakespeare's linguistic choices.

through Shakespeare's use of the semantic field of heroism and is described using the admirable adjectives of 'brave', 'noble' and 'worthy' throughout the beginning of act 1.

If a hero is to be seen as one who is considered to be admired for their 'brave' acts, or fine qualities, then we can most definitely assign this title to Macbeth in the early scenes, yet this title is fragile in its application. This is due to the fact that Macbeth is a duplicitous character. Whilst he is respected for his initial loyalty to his king and country, he is also seen to hold a 'vizard to [his] heart' through his wearing of his 'false face' as he privately liaises and fraternises with the supernatural spirits of the witches. This would alarm a contemporaneous audience as not only would this kind of deceptive behaviour be seen as treasonous, but his discussion and borderline obsession with the 'imperfect speakers' would set him in direct opposition to a heroic figure. Macbeth, as a 'noble' warrior should not be speaking to those who, by his own admission are 'imperfect', primarily as a result of the gender.

Whilst Macbeth appears to be interested in the witches' prophecies that state he will become 'Thane of Cawdor' and later 'King hereafter', his initial appetite for the regal status is cut short as he recognises that he should 'shut the door against [the king's murderer] not bear the knife [himself]'. This assertion comes after his acquisition of the title Thane of Cawdor where he questions 'why do you dress me in borrowed robes?' This question is interesting to explore as, whilst it may be rhetorical in nature, it may show his early submission to the disorder created by the supernatural as he could be seen to question a figure that does not appear to be present on stage. Whilst Macbeth may be in the early stages of his relationship with the witches, he is still of sound enough mind to refer to the 'robes' as 'borrowed', an adjective that clearly refers to the temporal nature of the robes that come to represent the role. This acknowledgement clearly parallels with the 'strange garments' that Banquo refers to which helps to demonstrate the disparity between the office (which is acutely represented through the clothing) and the man.

It is at this point that we must consider the ways in which Macbeth's heroism is indeed tragic and question whether he can be viewed as a tragic hero. It has been established that Macbeth has a keen sense of hubris in that he believes that he will become king as a result of the witches' initial prophecies despite him having to overcome the rule of primogeniture. Malcolm becoming the Prince of Cumberland is acknowledged by Macbeth as 'a step on which I must fall down, or else o'erleap, for in my way it lies'. Not only does Macbeth now realise that the king is still in power, making his reign seem impossible, but he also shows that he understands that Duncan's first-born son is the rightful heir in line to the throne. As such, Shakespeare uses Macbeth's hamartia of his submission to the supernatural's musings in order to warn the audience of the fatalistic dangers of

Do you think the candidate has begun to craft an argument yet?

The candidate understands how the context impacts on their understanding of the play's main ideas.

How does the candidate's use of short, embedded quotations enhance this response?

This focus on a specific moment in the play through detailed language analysis shows how confident this candidate is with the text and how they use this to support their overall ideas.

The candidate confidently explores the links between the task and the text here.

What is the effect of the candidate closing with the adverb 'initially' here?

committing regicide as we see Macbeth embark upon a journey that appears to mirror the tragic arc, initially.

Regicide is displayed within Shakespeare's play as an unthinkable act, one that is punishable by death and taboo in nature. This is supported by the fact that neither acts of regicide of both King Duncan and Macbeth are simulated on stage despite the unthinkable brutality of unashamed violence that is depicted across the remainder of the dramatic action. Macbeth, following his soliloquy of act 2, scene 1, concludes that Duncan should 'Hear it not [...]; for it is a knell, that summons thee to heaven or to hell'. Foolishly, Macbeth here appears to talk directly to the spirit of Duncan using the second person pronoun telling him it summons 'thee'. It is clear to an audience, however, the destination that Duncan will find himself travelling towards. He has shown himself to be a good king, with his only real failure being his failure to be with his army at the frontline, thus rendering him powerless to know the true reality of what happened there. A true tragic hero may well recognise the ramifications of their actions thus providing them with a moment of anagnorisis, yet Macbeth fails, even at this pivotal point within the play, to acknowledge that this 'knell' here is also summoning him to 'heaven or to hell'. It is worth acknowledging at this point, Shakespeare's intertextual reference to Donne's poem where he states that 'the bell tolls for thee'. The bell most definitely 'tolls' for Macbeth as it calls him to his fateful death.

Falling at a terrifying speed, Macbeth's descent into his role as the 'untitled tyrant' begins to pick up greater pace as his lust for ultimate power renders his once important friendships redundant to him. Macbeth becomes single-minded in his outlook and in act 3, scene 1 admits that 'our fears in Banquo stick deep'. His use of the possessive determiner 'our' here is interesting, as it is almost as though he is using his royal status to comment on how the whole of the country views Banquo at this point. Macbeth also admits that he has 'fears' regarding Banquo which, as the head of the state, suggests that he is attempting to discredit Banquo's nature, yet he only 'fears' his ability to expose him for his 'bloody deed[s]'. Furthermore, he uses the metaphor that these fears 'stick deep' another subtle admission that he is forever attached to his 'foul' play as for something to 'stick' it cannot be easily removed.

In the case of a true tragic hero, there is a sense of redemption as they potentially attempt to atone for their misgivings yet, in the case of Macbeth, this moment of anagnorisis never truly surfaces. Whilst Macbeth is shocked to discover that Macduff was from his 'mother's womb untimely ripped', this moment of recognition that his perceived protection from the witches' second set of prophecies has not borne fruit, does not truly conform to the tragic hero's moment of recognition. Macbeth never attempts to atone for his sins. There is, however, a moment of catharsis as Malcom is crowned 'King of Scotland!' at the close of the play, yet this could be viewed as Shakespeare's attempt to mirror life

---

The candidate shows a high level of engagement with the text here. They understand the impact of Shakespeare's dramatic choices.

The candidate returns to the main crux of the question here by supporting their argument with thoughtful references that are well explained.

How does the candidate develop their analysis successfully within this paragraph? Can you identify specific words used to do this?

The candidate rounds off their response successfully here by exploring whether the evidence that they have discussed across their answer supports their overall view in direct response to the question.

with art as he hopes for a more stable society for both the fictional characters of his play and the inhabitants of both Scotland and England under James I's rule.

Critical response

This response deals with a high-level concept that is more commonly suited to study at a more advanced level. The candidate understands the demands of the question and uses appropriate terminology and specific moments from the text to illustrate their ideas. There is an excellent understanding of context and this is convincingly discussed alongside the text rather than being covered in a stand-alone way. The candidate's use of references throughout the response show a deep level of engagement and the written style is personal and exploratory.

The marriage between Macbeth and Lady Macbeth

1.4 Starting with this extract, explore how Shakespeare presents the marriage between Macbeth and Lady Macbeth.

In the following extract from act 1, scene 7, Lady Macbeth and Macbeth are discussing their plans to kill King Duncan. Macbeth has told Lady Macbeth that he does not want to continue with the decision they previously made.

LADY MACBETH
What beast was't, then,
That made you break this enterprise to me?
When you durst do it, then you were a man;
And, to be more than what you were, you would
Be so much more the man. Nor time nor place
Did then adhere, and yet you would make both:
They have made themselves, and that their fitness now
Does unmake you. I have given suck, and know
How tender 'tis to love the babe that milks me:
I would, while it was smiling in my face,
Have pluck'd my nipple from his boneless gums,
And dash'd the brains out, had I so sworn as you
Have done to this.

MACBETH
If we should fail?

LADY MACBETH
We fail!
But screw your courage to the sticking-place,
And we'll not fail.

1.4.1 Critical response

The play's domesticity is surprising
Imagery from nature tells us home should be a safe haven; 'the poor wren' as opposed to the ominous 'raven'. The witches' twilight wren threatens the domestic household

Their marriage = the tragedy of childlessness, lots of focus on her state as a bereaved mother, but in the end her repressed femininity cannot be held off. She is rejected by her husband.

The marriage between the macbeths

wife should perform domestic duties

III.II
'Scorpions, dear wife'

V.V
'She should have died'

I.V
'Dearest partner I love'
'Duncan comes here tonight'

I.VII
Break promise we don't hear him make, Supports marriage encourage/goads him, Tragic role is unfulfilled

III.III
Your noble friends do lack you → tries to encourage him to bed – not for an explanation

Marriage for love, or marriage for status? Shakespeare's contemporaneous audience, and Shakespeare himself, would know all too well that a marriage was not often arranged based on love, but that love could develop within a marriage. It is unclear within Shakespeare's play how the marriage between the Macbeths came to be, yet what we can be certain of is that the marriage we see within this play is placed under Shakespeare's most extensive exploration. Whilst the marriage may not be an image of marital bliss, it does serve to explore the intimate relationship between two characters who do, despite potentially not ostensibly showing it in a traditional sense, love each other deeply and support each other through the tumultuous course of action that Macbeth chooses to pursue upon his return from war.

Whilst we can begin to form an image of the Macbeths' marriage early on in the play, we are left to do this without initially seeing them together. It is telling that Macbeth feels that he must write a letter to his wife to inform her of 'what greatness is promised thee' before he returns. It could be believed that Macbeth is as genuine as his words suggest; he wants her to know the 'greatness' that she will share with him, yet due to his duplicitous nature, it could be argued that he knows his wife well and anticipates that it is best to share this with her in a timely manner so that she can both digest the news, and potentially not chide him upon his return for not disclosing such alluring prophecies. Upon Macbeth's return, however, there is something reassuringly habitual about the way in which the Macbeths interact with one another. Macbeth refers to his wife as his 'dearest partner' within his letter and again as his 'dearest love' when

How has the candidate created a personal yet exploratory tone within their opening paragraph?

The analysis of text here is specific and focused. The candidate avoids making statements of certainty and instead explores the potential for multiple meanings.

Reference selection is judicious.

he physically returns to her. Whilst we cannot fail to consider the significance of the superlative 'dearest' as it suggests the hierarchical position that she occupies within his heart, the modulation of language from 'partner' to 'love' suggests something else entirely. The noun 'partner' holds connotations of equality; an arguably uncharacteristic feature of the Jacobean marriage, yet whilst his term of endearment 'love' may suggest that Macbeth holds romantic feelings towards his wife, it is more likely that this is an example of automated, even phatic, language. This conclusion can be reached as the Macbeths do not seem to express their joy at being reunited and instead, the 'partner'-like 'enterprise' upon which they plan to embark is set almost immediately in motion, removing any romantic sentiment which may have been present. Macbeth immediately informs his wife that 'Duncan comes here tonight' to which her response that she must 'provide' for him re-establishes her role as, ostensibly, the dutiful wife who performs domestic duties. This idea of the role of the supportive and obedient wife would curry favour with King James who set out the idea that a wife should be near to her husband at all times and be ready to obey his commands within his text *Basilikon Doron* published in 1603.

Arguably viewing herself as what King James would deem a good wife, Lady Macbeth obeys the traditional modus operandi of the wife and supports her husband in the marriage through both encouraging and goading him where she feels it necessary. This is most vociferously conveyed within act 1, scene 7 as Lady Macbeth challenges her husband by questioning 'what beast was it then, that made you break this enterprise to me?' As an audience, we do not witness Macbeth make this 'enterprise' and so we are left to question whether their marriage is one whereby their intuitive knowledge of one another leads us to question where he has made a promise to her, yet not in words. Interestingly, she charges the 'beast' with leading him to falter on his promise where this animalistic imagery could suggest that the fear he possesses here renders him wild and savage in that he does not conform to his role within the marriage. After all, it was commonly accepted that the husband would give commands and see them through. Despite Lady Macbeth often being viewed as 'fiend-like', there is a certain sadness in the way in which she expresses her frustration at her husband's initial refusal to stop Duncan seeing 'the sun' the next 'morrow'. Explaining how she has 'given suck, and know[s] How tender 'tis to love the babe that milks [her]', the real tragedy within this play could be seen to be that of their childless marriage. Lady Macbeth's language here is at odds with the common portrayal of her as a ruthless and vindictive counterpart to murder, instead she chooses to comment on how 'tender' this wholly maternal act between mother and child is. It is important to note that the more tender language within this scene precedes her admission that she 'would have dashed the brains out' where the modal verb 'would' allows an audience to recognise that this graphic image of violence is her responding to her husband in a language that he understands.

After all, he is famed and praised by the king for 'unseam[ing]' an enemy from the 'nave to the chaps' in the initial scenes.

Lady Macbeth's loyalty to her husband and their marriage ensues within act 3, scene 2, as she privately admits her own despair that 'all's spent, where our desire is got without content'. Yet it is significant that she never expresses her fears or doubts to him unlike he does to her. He confesses to her that 'full of scorpions is my mind, dear wife' where, again, the casual utterance of 'dear wife' seems to syntactically be an afterthought. This address term also serves to reveal that his entire mind is not occupied by 'scorpions'; a graphic metaphorical representation of his poisonous and dangerous thoughts, as he has still got the faculties available to tell his wife of his fears. Lady Macbeth never once reassures herself by agreeing that she too possesses these private fears. Instead, she supports her husband entirely by unhesitatingly supporting him throughout, reminding him that his 'noble friends do lack [him]' in act 3, scene 4 and by also taking the more dominant position within the marriage as she represses her femininity to protect him, despite not being aware of what is happening at this point, as she explains that his 'fit is momentary'.

What has the chronological writing style allowed this candidate to do so successfully within this response?

Significantly, as the communication between the Macbeths deteriorates beyond repair so too does their marriage. Macbeth's increasing secrecy is not a veil with which to protect his wife as he implores her to 'be innocent of the knowledge', but rather it serves to give him more power over her, and the country that he goes on to rule with the tyranny of a 'butcher'. Following his wife's death, who has shown herself to be loyal and attentive to her husband's needs, he can merely utter that 'she should have died hereafter'; a defining moment for Macbeth's character and their marriage. At this point, Macbeth has become nihilistic in his outlook and can only express his view that she would have died at some point as opposed to offering her the sentiments and care that she selflessly offered him throughout their life together.

This response concludes successfully as the candidate returns to their argument and offers a closing view that is cohesive and in line with what has been explored throughout the writing.

Critical response
This response has a clearly critical style that is developed through perceptive understanding and interpretation. The candidate starts confidently with a clear overall view about the Macbeths' marriage and then coherently exemplifies where and how this is demonstrated throughout their response. There is a clear sense of progression created through the chronological treatment of the text and references are precise, accurate and judicious throughout. This is a mature response that consistently handles the text and some complex ideas in a confident and assured way.

The role of a king

1.5 Starting with this extract, explore how Shakespeare presents the role of a king in *Macbeth*.

In the following extract from act 4 scene 3, Malcolm and Macduff are in England. They discuss Macbeth's reign over Scotland.

MALCOLM
Be not offended:
I speak not as in absolute fear of you.
I think our country sinks beneath the yoke;
It weeps, it bleeds; and each new day a gash
Is added to her wounds: I think withal
There would be hands uplifted in my right;
And here from gracious England have I offer
Of goodly thousands: but, for all this,
When I shall tread upon the tyrant's head,
Or wear it on my sword, yet my poor country
Shall have more vices than it had before,
More suffer and more sundry ways than ever,
By him that shall succeed.

MACDUFF
What should he be?

MALCOLM
It is myself I mean: in whom I know
All the particulars of vice so grafted
That, when they shall be open'd, black Macbeth
Will seem as pure as snow, and the poor state
Esteem him as a lamb, being compared
With my confineless harms.

MACDUFF
Not in the legions
Of horrid hell can come a devil more damn'd
In evils to top Macbeth.

MALCOLM
I grant him bloody,
Luxurious, avaricious, false, deceitful,
Sudden, malicious, smacking of every sin
That has a name: but there's no bottom, none,
In my voluptuousness: your wives, your daughters,

> Your matrons and your maids, could not fill up
> The cistern of my lust, and my desire
> All continent impediments would o'erbear
> That did oppose my will: better Macbeth
> Than such an one to reign.

1.5.1 Critical response

Role of a king inextricable to god's role and your worthiness to have contact with him. Divine right. Decisions and choices are God's and king is a vessel. Macbeth corrupts this = corrupt Scotland. WARNING. Basilikon Doran — James' beliefs

1 – Macbeth potential in 1.2–1.4	2 – Allows himself to be influenced act 1–2
His loyalty is to king and country, therefore could be ideal king. 'brave' 'noble' 'worthy' – contextual link to BD	Macbeth moves away from God and accepts supernatural influence of witches and Lady M. 'come you spirits' 'instruments of darkness'
3 – Extract + whole scene	4 – Extract = macbeth as unworthy
Chaos caused in Scotland as a result of macbeth's unworthy reign 'it weeps' 'a gash is added'	'black macbeth' = consumed by darkness 'hell' 'devil' 'sin' change in semantic field from start, no longer suitable

Inextricably bound to God, the role of a king is dictated by their position within the 'chain of being'. Whilst a king has power over their kingdom, that power is only given through God, and the commonly held belief by Jacobeans and James himself was that the king is only a vessel for God to communicate to his subjects, and it is here that Macbeth becomes unsuitable for the role. Macbeth wants the power to make decisions himself; he rejects God in his act of regicide and, therefore, cannot hold the role in any stable way. Shakespeare conforms to King James's views of kingship and utilises King James's views from the *Basilikon Doron*, evidently to pander to James as the play was, of course, written to be performed in court.

Loyal and respected in the opening scenes, Macbeth begins the play as a suitable candidate for kingship. It is through the perspective of other individuals that this version of Macbeth is given gravitas, particularly with Duncan himself confirming that Macbeth is 'worthy' and through him also being referred to as 'brave', 'valiant' and 'noble'. The trait of bravery positions Macbeth early on as willing to sacrifice himself in the battle to protect Scotland, and this solidifies him as someone who is loyal to king and country. This semantic field of kingship works in parallel with King James's *Basilikon Doron*, or the letter he wrote to his son, later published in England in 1603, which offers detailed instructions on how to be a good king, centred around the religious focus of the divine right of kings. Importantly, Macbeth has these qualities which are important within

How does the candidate begin with a focus on context?

This introduction sets out a clear focus on what a king's central role should be.

Judiciously selected evidence is used here to support the interpretation given.

How does the candidate develop the ideas from their introduction in this first paragraph?

Considers how the context of the text has influenced the ideas presented.

kingship, but unless he is chosen by God, he is not a worthy king. Shakespeare immediately highlights that the positive attributes of a leader are not enough: excellent morals and loyalty to the state may make you a good member of the court, but who is king only lies within God's power, not the realm of humanity.

The candidate's vocabulary here allows them to thoroughly develop a personal and specific interpretation.

Crucially, a king can only be influenced by themselves and God, but Macbeth allows far more – often supernatural – influences into his mind, and it is this that ultimately damns his potential as king. Easily manipulated by both his wife and the witches, the corrosive power of the supernatural leads Macbeth far from the potentially 'worthy' king he might be, and into a chaotic and destructive mindset that catapults him towards regicide. He pays no attention to Banquo's foreboding warning that the witches are 'instruments of darkness', or, more literally, tools of the devil, and allows himself to become another 'instrument' of chaos. Macbeth welcomes the darkness, as does Lady Macbeth, wanting to be covered in the 'dunnest smoke of Hell'. In choosing the side of the devil, Macbeth ultimately rejects the divine right of kings and, therefore, can no longer be a 'worthy' or 'noble' candidate for the role. This shunning of the natural order is established through Macbeth's reaction to the murder, when he claims that 'Amen stuck in my throat' – a clear sign that he has broken any connection he had with God in committing the most ungodly act and severing the state from its divine connection. Macbeth may recognise this too late, but a contemporaneous audience would not, this metaphorical verb 'stuck' being utilised by Shakespeare to display Macbeth's rejection of God, one that will lead to his rejection from the society of Scotland itself.

There are judicious and precise references picked here, used to make assured comments about the whole play.

Why is this comment on word analysis successful here?

How does the opening of this paragraph link to the previous idea?

The language analysis here is precise and focused and offers insightful ideas about the impact of Macbeth's position as king of Scotland.

By colluding with the devil, Macbeth's decision may bring him temporary power, but it only brings about the inevitable destruction of Scotland. This is most evident in act 4, scene 3, following the unnecessary 'slaughter' of Macduff's family, where Macduff and Malcolm discuss the tormented landscape of Scotland. We learn that the country 'weeps' and 'bleeds' and 'each new day a gash is added to her wounds'. The personification of the country with the feminine pronoun 'her' alludes to Scotland's weak and vulnerable status; it is as if Macbeth, as 'tyrant', is attacking and 'smacking' her and wounding the landscape. A king's duty to God is a duty to his kingdom and subjects, and James reasserts this in his letter to his son, where he reminds him to visit his subjects, however, it appears Macbeth's visits only lead to death, as 'each new day new widows howl', hinting at the limitless deaths Macbeth has brought to Scotland. It appears that the Macduff family massacre is not the only one, and Macbeth's ignorance of God is reaffirmed with Macduff's assertion that Macbeth's actions 'strike heaven on the face' – Macbeth not only rejects God's position in the hierarchy, but completely obliterates it and attempts to defile even heaven with his ungodly actions. Here Shakespeare is clear: a rejection of the king is a rejection of God – a dangerous path to lead in the God-fearing Jacobean England.

How are the comments made here, and the specific quotations picked, all linking back to the ideas established in the introduction?

Consumed by the darkness of the supernatural, Macbeth ends the play substantially different from the potentially king-like character of the opening scenes. The semantic field of heroism from the opening has been replaced by a semantic field of the purest evil; he is now associated with 'hell', the 'devil' and 'sin'. Macbeth's journey to the antithesis of a 'worthy' and 'noble' king has been exacted by not only his wife's influence, and the supernatural, but we must accept too his own 'black and deep desires' and his inability to see that he should retreat from the 'blood' he has 'stepped in' rather than continue to move forward. The density of religious language in act 4, scene 3 becomes heightened in the asyndetic listing of sins: 'bloody, luxurious, avaricious, false, deceitful'. These are sins that link explicitly to Macbeth's transgressions and offer a list of features to define him, juxtaposing our 'brave' warrior from act 1. Here, Shakespeare justifies the execution of a king, a fragile act to portray (interestingly, both Duncan's unlawful murder and Macbeth's justified murder occur off stage, perhaps a move sensitive to growing tension around King James's fragile reign) by listing his sins and associating him with the devil. Described through the stage direction of 'Re-enter Macduff, with Macbeth's head', the chaos within Scotland comes to an end, as with the death of Macbeth, and Malcolm's ascension, we realise that the natural order is restored. This is the ending made for King James, in a time of unstable kingship and assassination attempts, Shakespeare tells the court not to bother because God will always ensure that his chosen monarch will reign and that anyone countering the divine right will be severely punished.

> **Successful embedding of references here shows a comprehensive understanding of the whole play and considers how Macbeth's role has changed.**

> **What sophisticated terminology is used here to consider the effects created?**

> Various contexts – religious, moral, historical, social – are intertwined here to conclude the final critical argument in response to the play.

Critical response

This response is both confident and convincing, and the candidate has a thorough understanding of the role of kingship not only in the play, but in the contemporaneous society. The interpretation is founded on a strong contextual thread, which is weaved throughout, allowing the ideas to become exploratory and critical. In many ways the response's strengths lie with AO3 and AO1, but the analysis is still precise and detailed.

Appearance and reality

1.6 Starting with this extract, explore how Shakespeare presents ideas about appearance and reality in *Macbeth*.

In the following extract from act 1, scene 4, Duncan and Malcolm are discussing the former Thane of Cawdor. Macbeth and Banquo arrive following their encounter with the witches and Macbeth being given his new title.

DUNCAN
Is execution done on Cawdor? Are not
Those in commission yet return'd?

MALCOLM
My liege,
They are not yet come back. But I have spoke
With one that saw him die: who did report
That very frankly he confess'd his treasons,
Implored your highness' pardon and set forth
A deep repentance: nothing in his life
Became him like the leaving it; he died
As one that had been studied in his death
To throw away the dearest thing he owed,
As 'twere a careless trifle.

DUNCAN
There's no art
To find the mind's construction in the face:
He was a gentleman on whom I built
An absolute trust.
Enter MACBETH, BANQUO, ROSS, and ANGUS
O worthiest cousin!
The sin of my ingratitude even now
Was heavy on me: thou art so far before
That swiftest wing of recompense is slow
To overtake thee. Would thou hadst less deserved,
That the proportion both of thanks and payment
Might have been mine! only I have left to say,
More is thy due than more than all can pay.

MACBETH
The service and the loyalty I owe,
In doing it, pays itself. Your highness' part
Is to receive our duties; and our duties
Are to your throne and state children and servants,
Which do but what they should, by doing every thing
Safe toward your love and honour

1.6.1 Critical response

Play acts as a warning against blind acceptance — easy for macbeths to deceive initially, although all soon becomes clear (divine intervention?)	
1. Extract — theme established early 'no art to find the mind's construction in the face' — sets up ability to hide emotion, later established with Lady M and 'our duties are to your throne and state' (irony)	**2. macbeth and Lady macbeth transmitting deception in act 1** 'your face, my Thane, is as a book, where men may read strange matters' to 'innocent flower' to 'false face must hide what the false heart doth know'
3. Others begin to realise 2.3, 3.1 malcolm and Donalbain realise dangers (regicide hints at deception) — 'daggers in men's smiles' and Banquo is suspicious 'I feared thou playd'st most foully for it'	**4. Chaos grows — lose facade** Lady M sleepwalking in front of others, unable to decieve 'hell is murky' and visible blood (guilt) 'damned spot' and 'blood on thy face' in banquet (motif)

Dense with deception and riddled with facades, Shakespeare's *Macbeth* is a play that pivots on the appearance we present versus the reality we hide. Initially, it is easy for the Macbeths to deceive those in the court, but this facade crumbles as they ascend to power; the more they are placed under their self-initiated spotlight, the more their guilt is exposed. In this, Shakespeare warns against our blind acceptance of a person's loyalty, and in a time of treason and torture, the contemporaneous audience would do well to be honest and truthful to king and country.

Before Macbeth and Duncan are placed on stage together for the first time, Duncan himself raises the issue of deception and how easy it is to be deceived. He laments in act 1, scene 4 that 'There's no art to find the mind's construction in the face' – essentially, he had no way of knowing about the disloyal thoughts held by the previous Thane of Cawdor. Duncan notes the 'absolute trust' he placed on this traitor and, here, Shakespeare makes a clever dramatic decision. Macbeth enters, newly elevated and given this title, a title which is weighed down with the treasonous acts of its previous owner. Duncan's ignorance here is established with blatant dramatic irony; we have witnessed Macbeth soliloquise how 'murder yet is but fantastical' and consider how 'chance may crown' him. As Macbeth enters, we know that Duncan still cannot read the 'construction'

> Why is this a successful opening to the essay? Consider the phrasing used, as well as the ideas explored in this first paragraph.

> The extract is well-used here to support the candidate's own interpretation.

> In terms of analysis, the comments on dramatic methods show an awareness of staging and writer's craft, which are then successfully developed.

How do the comments on audience impact allow the candidate to develop their ideas?

Integrated references here are expertly chosen in order to explore the given theme. They offer close consideration of the question given.

How is the candidate showing a thorough understanding of the play at this point?

The candidate links their ideas together at this point, mentioning the ideas from the earlier paragraph and building on them.

The response offers exploratory comments on the way the Macbeths present themselves and, therefore, offers a detailed interpretation.

How does the essay here show a linking of analysis across the text? How is this successful?

of Macbeth's mind – an interesting metaphor suggesting that an individual can build an expression within their face that masks their true intentions. Saccharine and disingenuous, Macbeth's proclamation that 'our duties are to your throne and state' is also steeped in irony and contradicts the actions he is already considering. However, by allowing the audience to see these intentions, Shakespeare places us with more knowledge than the king, in order to warn us that it is easy to be deceived, even by those who act like they are incredibly loyal and trustworthy.

Shakespeare continues to tip the scales of appearance and reality throughout act 1 and 2, where Macbeth and Lady Macbeth play with the notion that they can hide their real intentions within a dutiful and obedient facade. Prior to literally telling Macbeth about how he should appear as an 'innocent flower' but behave internally like a 'serpent', Lady Macbeth warns him that his face 'is as a book, where men may read strange matters'. The metaphor of his face as a 'book', that the way he presents gives an obvious indication of his intentions, is most likely more indicative of Lady Macbeth's insecurity than of Macbeth's inability to hide his emotions. We have just watched Macbeth offer a false facade to Duncan, and then listen to the announcement of Malcolm to become Prince of Cumberland and therefore heir presumptive, and be able to remain composed enough that Duncan feels comfortable in visiting Macbeth's castle. Shakespeare utilises soliloquies in order to continue the theme and the deep dramatic irony; when witnessing the announcement Macbeth calls it a 'step', he must 'overleap' and reminds himself to 'hide' his 'black and deep desires'. Nevertheless, Macbeth does absorb Lady Macbeth's warning and instruction, as act 1 ends in his near repetition of her instruction, he tells himself 'false face must hide what false heart doth know', mirroring Duncan's earlier concerns of external deception, as well as the repetition of 'false' placing emphasis on the deceit that lies at the heart of the Macbeths' plans. Established as sinister and manipulative characters, Shakespeare draws our attention to the sheer cunning of villainous individuals, and the lengths they go to hide their 'black and deep desires'.

Once they commit regicide, both Macbeth and Lady Macbeth find it much more difficult to hide their intentions, and their sinister desires begin to manifest in interesting ways. With the murder of King Duncan, their carefully crafted plan to frame the guards appears to work on the majority of the assembled company, but their impulsive and reckless actions (far less planned) such as Macbeth killing the guards, and Lady Macbeth's feigned fainting, mean they tread on dangerous territory. Shakespeare establishes this through the reaction of Malcolm and Donalbain, who clearly do not believe it is the guards, and flee Scotland, with the final comment that 'There's daggers in men's smiles'. Again, Shakespeare utilises juxtaposition, mirroring Macbeth's earlier comments about 'face' and 'heart', but here with 'daggers' and 'smiles'. Here, we recall the saccharine comments of loyalty Macbeth offered and Donalbain acknowledges that many members of court offer smiles to their royal superiors but hide 'daggers' within them, a far more violent noun indicating the reality of deception hiding behind the 'false face' appearance. Suspicion is not exclusively held by the murdered king's sons, Banquo himself wants to talk more about the murder in act 2, scene 3, but then is given a soliloquy to open act 3 where his suspicions, specifically about Macbeth, are voiced. He has a 'fear' that Macbeth has 'playedst most foully' to secure the crown, and we now realise that the facade of loyalty and honour is not entirely faultless. It is here that the mask of the Macbeths begins to slip, with Shakespeare showing that their desperate hunt for power is ultimately what ruins them, because they place themselves in a spotlight from which there is no escape.

> By tracking the theme throughout the play, the candidate is able to show a detailed understanding of the play itself. They can also explore how the theme develops.

Metaphorically covering the Macbeths' hands from act 2, scene 2 onwards, the blood of their victims is what eventually leads to the Macbeths no longer being able to conceal their deceptive behaviour. We perhaps witness this as early as act 3, scene 4, where the murderer is told by Macbeth, 'there's blood on thy face', indicating that the murderer has entered the royal castle to visit the king with the blood of Banquo visible for everyone to see. This ties in with the motif of blood throughout and is representative of their metastasised guilt that permeates from this point onwards. Perhaps most obviously, this is highlighted in act 5, scene 1, where Lady Macbeth's face is much more than a 'book', and she vocalises their misdeeds for others to overhear. The 'spot' of blood that is stained on her 'little hand' ties in with Shakespeare's use of the motif, and it is the visibility of this moment which highlights how both of them are no longer able to maintain their deceptive facade, and by this point we might argue that Macbeth has made his cruel behaviour obvious, thus forcing Malcolm and Macduff to rally the troops in England and take back Scotland. Finally, Shakespeare helps us to realise that when the king and country are involved, deception will be unveiled, because God will not allow deception to rule over a kingdom. However, as individuals, we should take heed of the deceptive influence of the individuals (like Guy Fawkes) who might not have our best interests, or the interests of the state, at the forefront of their minds.

> **Why is this a exploratory point? How does this ensure the paragraph starts in an engaging way?**

> Exploring the motif of blood in relation to appearance and reality allows the candidate to show an excellent knowledge of the entire play.

> These closing comments allow the candidate to consider the contextual implications beyond the play itself.

Critical response
This response is largely successful because of the precise references which all relate to the theme in question. The quotations picked form an integral part of the response, and they are embedded seamlessly into the argument, allowing the candidate to explore the text thoroughly. Furthermore, these precise references are analysed with considerable attention, and the candidate considers context by focusing on the monarchy and kingship, and the way the play would be received. It is an exploratory, thorough, and critical response.

A Christmas Carol

Suffering of the poor

2.1 Starting with this extract, explore how Dickens presents the suffering of the poor in *A Christmas Carol.*

In this extract from stave one, we are told of Scrooge and Bob's situation at work. Scrooge is then visited by his nephew, Fred.

> The door of Scrooge's counting-house was open that he might keep his eye upon his clerk, who in a dismal little cell beyond, a sort of tank, was copying letters. Scrooge had a very small fire, but the clerk's fire was so very much smaller that it looked like one coal. But he couldn't replenish it, for Scrooge kept the coal-box in his own room; and so surely as the clerk came in with the shovel, the master predicted that it would be necessary for them to part. Wherefore the clerk put on his white comforter, and tried to warm himself at the candle; in which effort, not being a man of a strong imagination, he failed.
> 'A merry Christmas, uncle! God save you!' cried a cheerful voice. It was the voice of Scrooge's nephew, who came upon him so quickly that this was the first intimation he had of his approach.
> 'Bah!' said Scrooge, 'Humbug!'
> He had so heated himself with rapid walking in the fog and frost, this nephew of Scrooge's, that he was all in a glow; his face was ruddy and handsome; his eyes sparkled, and his breath smoked again.
> 'Christmas a humbug, uncle!' said Scrooge's nephew. 'You don't mean that, I am sure?'
> 'I do,' said Scrooge. 'Merry Christmas! What right have you to be merry? What reason have you to be merry? You're poor enough.'
> 'Come, then,' returned the nephew gaily. 'What right have you to be dismal? What reason have you to be morose? You're rich enough.'

2.1.1 Clear response

'Keep an eye upon his clerk […] in a dismal little cell beyond'	Are there no prisons?' 'And the union workhouse?'
'nobody said or thought it was at all a small pudding for a large family' 'tell me if Tiny Tim will live'	I'll raise your salary, and endeavour to assist your struggling family 'second father'

This response opens with a comment on Dickens' purpose showing that the candidate understands the context and main ideas of the text.

In *A Christmas Carol*, Charles Dickens shows us the large contrast between those who live in poverty and those who are wealthier. Poverty and wealth live side by side within Victorian London and Dickens attempts to educate readers on the need to look at themselves to ensure that they are not treating the poor in the same way Scrooge does at the beginning of the novella.

In stave one, we are told that Scrooge keeps the door of his counting house open so that he can 'keep an eye upon his clerk'. This could suggest that Scrooge is suspicious of the work that Bob Cratchit does and might not trust him with the money in the counting house, even though Bob would have been very grateful to have found a job in the first place. The narrator then explains that Bob works in a 'dismal little cell', which has connotations of the office being like a prison. These two quotations link because it is almost as though Scrooge does not want to trust Bob and thinks that just because he is poor, he is similar to a criminal. This is why Dickens chooses the noun 'cell' as it reveals that Bob is locked up by Scrooge, and Dickens shows us that this negative view was the one that was often held by the wealthy people in society. This may have made the readers of the novel question if they too treated those in poverty like Scrooge as Dickens was trying to discourage this unfair treatment.

We hear Scrooge's miserable and misanthropic voice when he questions the charity collectors using two rhetorical questions one after the other. He asks 'Are there no prions?', followed by 'And the union workhouse?' Scrooge is an educated man and knows that these terrible places were open and many poor people found themselves within them sometimes through no fault of their own. He doesn't really question the charity collectors instead, he just tries to suggest that the charity collectors should send poor people to 'prison or the 'workhouse' as he 'can't afford to make idle people merry', which is ironic because we know that Scrooge is a rich man who owns his own company and can hire an employee to work for him.

As the novel develops, Scrooge is not making rapid progress towards changing his view of those living in poverty. Dickens has to choose a stronger method to make Scrooge realise that his lifestyle and views are damaging to both himself and society. In stave three, the Ghost of Christmas Present takes Scrooge to Bob Cratchit's house where he watches from the window as Bob and his family celebrate Christmas. This already shows the difference between Scrooge and Bob. Scrooge does not want to celebrate Christmas and thinks Bob has over-stepped the mark when he asks for Christmas day off in the first place. This could also be Dickens showing that Scrooge is not a good Christian because he does not celebrate the most important day in the Christian calendar. This shows that Scrooge is unlikely to have the strong morals that Dickens wanted people in society to have so that they could help one another. The Christmas dinner is not large, but 'nobody said or thought it was at all a small pudding for a large family'. The juxtaposition here shows that despite the fact the pudding is only 'small', the hearts of the Cratchits are 'large', which shows that you can make a choice to see the best in things if you choose to. At the end of this stave, Scrooge asks the ghost to 'tell me if Tiny Time will live'. This is the first time that Scrooge has

What do you notice about the way the candidate includes their evidence?

The candidate strengthens their response by linking evidence together to support their overall idea in this paragraph.

How does the candidate use their vocabulary here to support their response?

Using the phrase 'as the novel develops' signifies that the candidate is aware of the structure of the text and how ideas can progress and change.

How could the candidate have made the opening of this paragraph more analytical instead of explanatory?

Supported understanding of how change is shown through careful selection of evidence.

really asked after someone other than himself, which shows that he cares for the welfare of Bob's son. This allows Dickens to show that Scrooge is beginning to change how he acts towards others.

At the end of the novel, Dickens presents Scrooge to the reader as a changed man. Scrooge says to Bob that he will 'raise your salary, and endeavour to assist your struggling family' and the verb 'assist' shows that Scrooge is ready to try to help others. If everyone who read the novel who had previously acted in a similar way to Scrooge attempted to change their ways and help others, then Dickens' aim of the novel would have been achieved and there would not be such a large gap between the rich and poor of society. Dickens allows us to see that Scrooge changes in more than just the way he sees money at the end too as he becomes a 'second father' to Tiny Tim, showing that he also shares his love as well as his money. This ultimately makes Scrooge a happier individual and shows the warm power that love can have.

Clear response

This response is a clear one in that it addresses the task given and methodically works its way through the novel to provide evidence as to how the suffering of the poor is presented as the novel develops. Explanations of the methods used are clearly understood with terminology used accurately to enhance the response. The candidate starts to draw links between specific moments and pieces of evidence within the text and all ideas are supported by comments that show an understanding of the context and the intentions of the author.

2.1.2 Thoughtful response

Within *A Christmas Carol*, Dickens uses the text to convey a powerful message that not all those who find themselves living in poverty are criminals and vagabonds. Moreover, Dickens employs the Cratchit family to embody the struggles of the poor giving them a generous presentation and showing how attitudes to the poor in Victorian England could, and needed to, change.

At the start of the novella, we are introduced to Scrooge who is shown to have an incredibly negative attitude towards those living in poverty. His own clerk, Bob Cratchit is seen to work in the room next door to him which is described as a 'dismal little cell'. The noun 'cell' presents the idea that even though Bob Cratchit has a job (which many people would have thought of as a privilege) he is also trapped within his job in a kind of prison. This could suggest that the poor, who struggled to find employment, were treated poorly by those of a higher class, often being treated as criminals and working in harsh conditions as a result of the lack of care the higher classes showed to them. It is almost as though Dickens wants the reader to imagine how bad the treatment of the poor was and, for many, living in a 'cell', in prison, is the worst consequence many can think of.

Clear topic sentences help this candidate to present their point before explaining how this is achieved.

How does the candidate link their closing ideas to their opening ideas so that their response is cohesive?

Succinctly, the candidate has outlined their understanding of the writer's ideas, context and main message. This shows confidence with the text.

What does the candidate's use of the phrase 'it is almost as though' help them to suggest and do here?

The character of Scrooge represents the miserly capitalists of the early 19th century and Dickens shows the view of this group of people when Scrooge is approached by the charity collectors. Scrooge asks the charity collectors two rhetorical questions; 'are there no prisons?'; 'and the union workhouses?' Scrooge asks these questions to two men who are 'endeavouring' to help those who are less fortunate, yet Scrooge does not need to ask these questions as he already knows the answers – both of these institutions were in 'full vigour'. It is Scrooge's hatred for the poor that is shown by these rhetorical questions as he believes that if they could not support themselves then they should go to 'prison' or a 'workhouse'. As a 'prison' is a place for criminals to serve their punishment, this suggests that Scrooge (and others of his class) believe that being poor is a crime in itself and deserves to be punished. Worse than that, his suggestion that the poor could go to a 'workhouse' also shows his lack of understanding of the struggles of the poor as many would rather die than go to a workhouse and endure the harsh conditions and risk being separated from their families. This also shows that, at the start of the novella, Scrooge does not understand the value of family and love to those living in poverty, such as Bob Cratchit and his little family as they would 'rather die' than go to a workhouse alone.

Within stave three, Dickens uses the Ghost of Christmas Present to take Scrooge to see the Cratchit family who are desperately poor and a 'struggling family'. In this stave, Scrooge sees Bob's son Tiny Tim for the first time and appears to take an interest in him after watching him at the table as he toasts 'God bless us, everyone'. This religious language shows that whilst the Cratchits do not have much, they do have faith and in a Christian society, this would have been important to many and so it is almost as though Dickens includes this so that the Cratchits would have been viewed as respectable despite their poverty. This also shows them as a contrast to Scrooge who is seen as an 'old sinner'. Scrooge asks the spirit to 'tell me if Tiny Tim will live' where Dickens shows us that Scrooge is changing his attitude towards the poorest in society – a clear message for others to do the same – as before he didn't understand the poor and just saw them as the 'surplus population'. Specifically, the adjective 'surplus' shows that Scrooge saw the poor as unnecessary extras and not vital to society.

Scrooge's drastic change in view is presented in the extract at the end of stave three as we are shown the figures of Ignorance and Want, who command Scrooge to 'beware' using an imperative verb. These figures clearly show the struggles of the poor as they are presented using zoomorphism, which suggests that the poor were often treated like animals instead of like humans. Scrooge asks if he sees a 'foot or a claw' showing that these children have unrecognisable bodies – they are presented as 'yellow, meagre, ragged, scowling, wolfish'. This list of negative adjectives shows just how badly these children had been treated. Specifically, the adjective 'scowling' could suggest how angry they are at how they have been treated and they are 'meagre' like unfed animals. In a change

The candidate here shows that they understand methods that are beyond language devices. By understanding that the characters are representative of larger ideas shows the thoughtful confidence of the candidate.

Consider how many drop quotations the candidate uses in this paragraph. What is the effect of these?

By working through the text chronologically, the candidate is able to show the development of characters and ideas.

Method analysis supported by a thoughtful understanding of the context helps to strengthen points made.

Judicious choices of references support close analysis of the text here.

How does the candidate ensure that their response ends cohesively here?

to stave one, Scrooge asks 'have they no refuge or resource?', which is different to the rhetorical questions he asked before – this time he genuinely wants to know if these poor children can have help. It is almost as though Dickens wants to show the reader the changing attitudes of a man like Scrooge to convey that if someone who has such negative views as Scrooge can change his ways then so can anyone.

> **Thoughtful response**
> This response has an appropriately developed, thoughtful style with precise and well-chosen references embedded throughout. Ideas are discussed thoroughly that allows analysis to go beyond surface level, which is enhanced by the candidate's understanding that the writer's methods are not just language based. There is a strong awareness of the impact that the text intended to have on readers and sensitive consideration is given to the context of the novel that supports the analysis.

2.1.3 Critical response

The vocabulary used in this opening shows that the candidate is crafting their ideas and is highly confident with the subject matter.

Within his allegorical novella, *A Christmas Carol*, Dickens highlights the plight of the poor through his presentation of several of the characters. Dickens specifically conveys the treatment and suffering of the poor through the way the central protagonist, Scrooge, interacts with those who have been touched by the cruel hand of poverty, and also through his changing ideas about how the poor should be treated. Ultimately, Dickens presents the suffering of the poor to provide his readers with a moral lesson; those in poverty are no better or worse than those who do not find themselves in such 'frightful' and 'wretched' conditions. This is a message pertinent to both modern and contemporaneous readers.

The treatment of the text here is assured. The candidate is able to speculate on detail that may be overlooked had they not had such a strong understanding of the historical context of the text.

It becomes clear in stave one that it is undeniable that Scrooge has a difficult relationship with both himself and others. Whilst working in a 'cramped' counting house, his clerk, Bob Cratchit works in what is described as a 'dismal little cell'. Embodying those in poverty, Cratchit belongs to the deserving poor – those in Victorian Britain who, despite their best efforts to engage in employment, still found themselves unable to provide for their 'struggling famil[ies]'. It is this nuance that Dickens may be trying to highlight here. It is incredibly damaging and dangerous to label all those in poverty as 'idle', yet it is this blinkered treatment of the poor as a whole that Scrooge falls foul of. By keeping his clerk working in a 'cell', which has clear connotations of incarceration, there is the suggestion that even when engaged in lawful employment that employers who would often be of a higher social status still treated their employees as criminals. However, there is potentially more to this. Not only are the poor, like Bob Cratchit, imprisoned within their physical surroundings, but they are also caged by a much larger yet invisible trap – society's view of them. It is almost as though Dickens seeks to demonstrate that those living in poverty will never be truly liberated until those privileged

How does the candidate build layers into their analysis within this paragraph?

members of any society, like Scrooge, can change their global view of the poor and 'endeavour' to embrace and support them.

It is difficult to imagine that such callous treatment of 'fellow passengers to the grave' is something that always lived within Scrooge, and other characters of his ilk. As such, it is interesting to consider where Scrooge's view of the poor stems from. Within stave one itself, Scrooge is described through the simile 'as hard and sharp as flint', which could be seen to suggest that Scrooge is simply that: hard and of a similar density to a rock. However, the chremamorphism here also suggests that like a 'flint', Scrooge is capable of producing fire, of producing warmth moreover. The act of creating fire in early civilisation allowed human activity to continue into the dark and colder hours of the day which not only suggests that it is characters like Scrooge who have the ability to provide light and warmth, but it is them who can metaphorically lengthen the days and alleviate the darkness of people's lives. Despite a reader being told that 'darkness is cheap and Scrooge liked it' in stave one, we must consider whether the view of the narrative voice at this point is wholly accurate and whether Scrooge does indeed 'like' the darkness of his 'oyster' shell. Within stave two, we see the figure of Scrooge as a younger man who comments that 'There is nothing on which [the world] is so hard as poverty' which is telling. As Dickens would well have known, poverty made life incredibly challenging for so many. Therefore, this comment from a younger Scrooge may hint at reasons why he appears to dislike the poor so much. The question raised at this point then is whether Scrooge's fears of poverty are made manifest as a dislike of the poor rather than poverty itself. It could therefore be suggested that Scrooge so fears the suffering that he experienced as a 'solitary child' that he protects himself through a coldness that ensures that he does not open himself to a world of hurt once again. He does indeed 'fear the world too much'.

Dickens presents the suffering of the poor clearly through the Cratchits who are first introduced in stave three. Despite the family's 'twice turned' clothes and 'threadbare' accessories, their warmth and bond are a stark contrast to Scrooge's own cold and isolated life. Despite suffering financially, they do not suffer emotionally and it is, at this point, where we must consider whether Dickens is awakening a reader to the idea that financial and emotional poverty are both causing suffering in their different ways. In this stave, Scrooge takes a keen interest in Tiny Tim as he toasts 'God bless us, everyone '. This religious language shows that whilst the Cratchits do not have much, as well as having each other they also have faith. To locate this in a Christian context, this would have allowed a wealthier reader to acknowledge the good within the Cratchits as God-fearing people, yet on another level, their faith also allows them to also believe in the 'founder of the feast'. It is this Christian hope and understanding which ultimately ends Scrooge's own emotional poverty as he awakens in stave five as a changed man after seeing the spirit of the Cratchits. Prior to his 'amends', Scrooge asks the spirit to 'tell [him] if Tiny Tim will live ' where

Ideas seamlessly move from the micro to the macro.

The candidate starts to consider more conceptual ideas here.

How does the candidate's attempt to look for multiple layers of meaning here enhance their response?

The personal yet critical style of writing here shows an insightful engagement with the text and its ideas.

Sustained discussion of ideas here link with earlier points raised in the essay.

How does the candidate continue to refer to the writer's intentions throughout? What is the overall effect of this?

Dickens shows us that Scrooge is changing his attitude towards the poorest in society – a clear message for others to do the same – as before he didn't understand the poor and just saw them as the 'surplus population'. Specifically, the adjective 'surplus' shows that Scrooge saw the poor as unnecessary extras and not vital to society.

The method analysis here is precise and detailed. The candidate analyses the language against the backdrop of extensive contextual knowledge to show that they understand the important significance of Dickens' ideas.

Scrooge's drastic change in view is presented in the extract at the end of stave three as we, and Scrooge, are shown the figures of Ignorance and Want, who the spirit commands Scrooge to 'beware' using an imperative verb. These figures clearly show the struggles of the industrial poor and Dickens' use of zoomorphism could suggest that the poor were often treated like animals instead of like humans. Scrooge asks if he sees a 'foot or a claw' showing that these children have unrecognisable bodies as he must clarify what he thinks he sees. The children are presented as 'yellow, meagre, ragged, scowling, wolfish' where this asyndetic list of pejorative adjectives shows just how badly these children have been treated. Specifically, the adjective 'wolfish' could suggest that these figures are presented to Scrooge by Dickens in order to teach him a lesson. Within European literature, the wolf was often employed to represent the figure of a teacher, albeit the lesson that was often taught was a difficult one to digest. This could reveal that Dickens was aware that in order for men like Scrooge to transform their attitudes they must be taught a lesson that would not only shock them but would enable them to critically evaluate themselves. Evidence of this lesson working comes in the form of the question 'have they no refuge or resource?'. Whilst similar to the questions posed in stave one, it is actually widely different as this time he genuinely wants to know if these poor children can be helped. His language modulates from one concerned with productivity and labour, to one of support and a socialist outlook. It is in this moment, surrounded again by children, that Scrooge recognises that they are the future of society and without a change in his and other's ways, they will never 'profit' or prosper and he will never again see a 'spring-time in the haggard winter of his life'.

The candidate does not cover the entirety of the text. Do you think this is necessary to show a full understanding of the novel's ideas?

Critical response

This response consistently handles the text and its question with sustained confidence. Much reference is made to contextual factors that act as a backdrop to the content of the novel and the candidate's understanding of these elements and careful explanation of them supports the analysis fully. The candidate's written style is fluent and mature as they choose to use extensive vocabulary and assume an examiner's understanding. The response is sustained in its development and references are judiciously chosen and explored well to exemplify ideas. This response does not cover the whole text, yet this does not mar the quality of the response provided, although this is something for consideration moving forward at this level.

Scrooge's relationships with others

2.2 Starting with this extract, explore how Dickens presents Scrooge's relationships with others in *A Christmas Carol.*

'Don't be cross, uncle!' said the nephew.

'What else can I be,' returned the uncle, 'when I live in such a world of fools as this? Merry Christmas! Out upon merry Christmas! What's Christmas time to you but a time for paying bills without money; a time for finding yourself a year older, but not an hour richer; a time for balancing your books and having every item in 'em through a round dozen of months presented dead against you? If I could work my will,' said Scrooge indignantly, 'every idiot who goes about with 'Merry Christmas' on his lips, should be boiled with his own pudding, and buried with a stake of holly through his heart. He should!'

'Uncle!' pleaded the nephew.

'Nephew!' returned the uncle sternly, 'keep Christmas in your own way, and let me keep it in mine.'

'Keep it!' repeated Scrooge's nephew. 'But you don't keep it.'

'Let me leave it alone, then,' said Scrooge. 'Much good may it do you! Much good it has ever done you!'

'There are many things from which I might have derived good, by which I have not profited, I dare say,' returned the nephew. 'Christmas among the rest. But I am sure I have always thought of Christmas time, when it has come round—apart from the veneration due to its sacred name and origin, if anything belonging to it can be apart from that—as a good time; a kind, forgiving, charitable, pleasant time; the only time I know of, in the long calendar of the year, when men and women seem by one consent to open their shut-up hearts freely, and to think of people below them as if they really were fellow-passengers to the grave, and not another race of creatures bound on other journeys. And therefore, uncle, though it has never put a scrap of gold or silver in my pocket, I believe that it has done me good, and will do me good; and I say, God bless it!'

The clerk in the Tank involuntarily applauded. Becoming immediately sensible of the impropriety, he poked the fire, and extinguished the last frail spark for ever.

'Let me hear another sound from you,' said Scrooge, 'and you'll keep your Christmas by losing your situation! You're quite a powerful speaker, sir,' he added, turning to his nephew. 'I wonder you don't go into Parliament.'

2.2.1 Clear response

Scrooge's relationships with others represent his relationships with wider society. Change in relationship = change in perspective.	
1 Relationship with Bob/Fred at the start	**2 Relationship with the poor**
Rude and abrupt with both – family or not – threatens Bob openly 'lose your situation' and mocks Fred 'world of fools'	'are there no prisons' 'decrease the surplus population' doesn't see them as human, unnecessary burden
3 Past relationships	**4 Relationship changes by end**
memories remind him of actual love affection he lost. Fan + Belle + Fezziwig 'another idol has displaced me'	'light as a feather' – relieved of burden of his behaviour towards others, or potential chains like marley, 'second father'

How is the candidate's idea clear from this opening sentence?

At times, this paragraph can seem slightly narrative, as they are trying to cover various ideas from the extract. Their ideas are clear, although not well-developed, at this point.

At the start of the novella, Scrooge is presented as a cruel and misanthropic miser who rejects human company and kindness. At this moment in stave one, we get a real glimpse of how he engages with others, and his treatment of both his nephew, Fred, and his employee Bob, is quite similar: he is rude and abrupt, saying that he lives in a 'world of fools'. He is calling his own nephew, present in the conversation and only there to offer him a place for Christmas dinner, a 'fool' for wanting to enjoy Christmas. When Bob applauds Fred's speech, Scrooge threatens Bob that he will 'lose your situation!' with the exclamation mark here hinting at Scrooge's angry tone and his increasing frustration with both Fred and Bob in their attempts to be positive about Christmas. Scrooge's mocking of those he is around, who only show him kindness, and his angry responses to them, represent how he interacts with all of the people in his life. Dickens establishes Scrooge in this way early on to encourage the Victorian reader to immediately see him as cruel and dislike the way he interacts with others, and in doing so, Dickens discourages the reader from behaving in a similar way.

What other evidence could be used here to prove this idea?

We soon learn that Scrooge's behaviour is even worse when it comes to the nameless poor of Victorian London. Rather than the abrupt and blunt mocking he gives Fred and Bob, he is completely cruel and heartless when discussing how to treat the poor with the two charity collectors. When asked for a contribution Scrooge replies with 'are there no prisons?'. This rhetorical question (he knows that there are) highlights Scrooge's view on those in poverty – that they should be punished and be forced into either a prison or a 'workhouse' so that they can repent for their crime of being poor. We realise, as the novella progresses, that the reality is that Scrooge has no knowledge of a life of poverty, and he must be reminded of his own childhood and then be forced to watch the Cratchits to realise those in poverty are not 'idle people' but often kind and loving human beings who want the best for their family. This is Dickens' key message to the reader: that the poor are underestimated and undervalued by those with money,

How does the link to the rest of the novella here help to show the candidate's strong knowledge?

and they should look at the reality of the lower-class lifestyle, as this will make those with money realise that they should contribute and support people who work hard but still have so little and have a better relationship with the people who suffer in Victorian England.

When Scrooge is forced to relive his past memories, he is reminded of relationships where he felt genuine love and affection. It is clear that Scrooge has decided to purposefully forget these memories, so having to see his sister Fan, his ex-fiancée Belle, and his former boss Fezziwig brings out a range of emotions, very different to the anger that he feels towards others in stave one. The memory of Belle breaking off the engagement is an important one, and Scrooge calls it 'torture', as he is forced to watch the moment where his most important relationship is lost to the 'golden idol' Belle feels has 'displaced' her. These memories of relationships, which Scrooge actually wanted, force him to reconsider how he engages with others. The metaphor of the 'golden idol' is crucial: Scrooge once chose this 'idol', or money, over his connection with Belle, and now he continues to do this by opting for higher wealth over enjoying Christmas or contributing to charity. These selfish actions are highlighted because in this memory he sees the repercussions of those choices, and begs the spirit to end the memory, highlighting his emotional reaction. Dickens wants to show the bleak reality of a life that chooses money over love: it is clear that Scrooge's loneliness is a result of his choices, rather than an actual choice, and he must remember these moments in order to realise this.

Each ghost encourages a change in Scrooge, and by the end, he decides to change the relationships he has with others as he realises the mistakes of his past and present. Scrooge reconciles with Fred by attending his Christmas dinner, paying the money to charity, and raises Bob's wages, providing for the Cratchit family. Scrooge wakes up and feels 'as light as a feather', and this simile highlights that a weight has been lifted from Scrooge when he decides to change. The pressure of being misanthropic towards others has resulted in a sad, lonely death, and Scrooge is ready to lift that burden from himself and become light and free, with the noun 'feather' showing a sense of freedom and liberation. Scrooge also becomes a 'second father' to Tiny Tim, and in doing so begins to build real human relationships and connections with those around him. Dickens reminds us that it's never too late to become a better person, and to interact not only with those in our family but anyone we meet, and anyone in society who needs us. Ultimately, Dickens wants his Victorian reader, particularly the businessmen with money, to accept that this is how they should behave, and encourage them to be like the Scrooge at the end of the novella rather than the misanthropic Scrooge we meet in the opening pages.

2.2.2 Thoughtful response

In Dickens' *A Christmas Carol*, we see Scrooge transform from a misanthropic and avaricious man to an individual who opts for philanthropy and builds genuine connections with others. Across the novella, we realise that each one of his relationships represents his understanding of society and his role in it in presenting this change, Dickens advocates for a change in all Victorian businessmen who may forge relationships that are about money rather than compassion.

Undeniably filled with resentment and bitterness, we immediately see Scrooge's lack of connection with those around him in stave one. Scrooge's relationship with Bob and Fred appears simple: he is cruel and rude, and this is how he treats everyone. When Scrooge describes a 'world of fools', this hyperbolic reaction highlights how he groups everyone in the same way: everyone in society lacks knowledge and are, therefore, 'fools'. For Scrooge, this justifies his misanthropic attitude – he chooses not to spend time with others because they are mere 'fools'. This lack of connection is reinforced in how he interacts with Bob in the extract, with his threat to Bob that he will 'lose your situation'. In truth, Scrooge's lack of connection with Bob is actually due to his ignorance about Bob's life and his inability to empathise with Bob's current 'situation'. Scrooge does not realise the impact that Bob losing his job would have on the Cratchit family, and so his understanding of the poor and the wider society is limited to the 'narrow limits' he sets for himself. We quickly realise that whilst Scrooge fundamentally believes that everyone else is an ignorant 'fool', he is wrong, and in fact, *he* is ignorant. Dickens' attempt to reinforce this early on is aimed at his contemporaneous reader, who might ask themselves if Scrooge's view of society is correct – if he lives in a 'world of fools' that extends to everyone. Of course, the real irony here is that Scrooge is the only fool as he is unable to understand his own ignorance.

Scrooge's avarice is the central motivation behind the relationship he has with those in penury. He does not attempt to create genuine, compassionate relationships at the start of the novella, because he does not believe there is any gain or value in those who are poor. When he speaks to the charity collectors and asks 'are there no prisons?'. His views on the poor are evident – they are criminals. He dehumanises the poor because he himself is afraid of poverty (as discussed with Belle in stave two) and this fear is what motivates him to view the poor as a collective who deserve the horror of 'prisons' and 'workhouses'. Additionally, the business-like language with which he refers to the poor is indicative of his lack of compassion and connection with them. He calls the poor the 'surplus population', with the financially-motivated adjective of 'surplus' revealing that he sees the poor as a product of our society, rather than actual humans who deserve kindness. This dehumanisation of the poor reflects Scrooge's wider relationship with society; in referring to the poor as only 'surplus' he can justify the way he treats them and his decision to not offer them support. Dickens offers this as a criticism of those who are motivated by money only – it is Scrooge's avarice that forces the poor to the 'prisons' and 'workhouses', and this symbolises the actions of many others in Victorian society.

Scrooge's past relationships eventually motivate him to reflect on the lack of connection he has created in his present existence. The Ghost of Christmas Past exposes Scrooge to relationships that he has clearly repressed, and in his pursuit of wealth and solitude, he has forgotten the lessons he could have learnt from these relationships. Key individuals in his former years such as Fan, Fezziwig and Belle, all offer him a genuine connection, but ones that he has lost and been unable to create, leaving him a lonely individual. Crucially, his relationship with Belle and his reaction to their end of 'contract', begin to force Scrooge into considering his relationships with others. When Belle tells the younger Scrooge 'another idol has displaced me', we are again shown how Scrooge has spent his life choosing money over connections, and this has resulted in a man who has no relationships with others. The metaphor of money as an 'idol' is interesting, as it highlights how Scrooge does create a relationship, but it is only with wealth, which he worships, almost like his only faith is in what money can offer him. Scrooge struggles to watch these memories, highlighting a change, and by the start of stave three, he mentions that he is being taught a 'lesson' which is 'working'. This awareness of a need to learn and change reinforces to the reader the change that Dickens is advocating: that we all create healthy and kind connections, both with those in our immediate circle, and the wider society.

Finally, by the end of the novella, we learn that Scrooge has not only changed his relationships with others but also that he has created long-lasting and genuine connections with those around him and his wider community. He becomes one of the best people the 'good old city' of London has ever had and becomes a 'second father' to Tiny Tim. Dickens' use of a familial metaphor here establishes that Scrooge's new relationship with Tim is not false or motivated by a selfish desire to not carry a chain like Marley, but instead is a true connection and desire to make Tim's life better, like the unconditional affection a father might feel for their child. Furthermore, the simile utilised by Dickens highlights

There is a confident and considered knowledge of the text. This paragraph pulls in various comments made by Scrooge in stave 1 to support the point being made.

Why might the candidate have chosen to explain the narrative at this point? Could they have been more precise here?

There is thoughtful consideration of Dickens' purpose here. Rather than focusing on social context, they consider the big ideas around the text.

There are some thoughtful analytical comments made in this paragraph. It considers both the metaphor and simile and the various effects achieved.

how Scrooge has realised the burden of misanthropy, as he is now 'as light as a feather', metaphorically releasing the weight of his solitary and lonely life, and having a different view of his purpose in life. Scrooge is now living by Marley's mantra: 'mankind' becomes Scrooge's 'business', as does kindness and compassion, and Dickens reinforces this in the final chapter with the extreme change in Scrooge, which we know is not only temporary – something that Dickens hopes for his reader to emanate to make Victorian Britain a better place for those who struggle most.

> **Thoughtful response**
> This response is particularly successful with regards to its AO1; the references are well integrated into the response, and the knowledge of text is extremely secure. This allows the answer to take an overall approach to the task, and its explanation is considered and confident. It's AO3 is covered with some consideration of the bigger ideas within the text rather than a focus throughout on social or historical context. The response would benefit from some deeper analysis of language or structure.

2.2.3 Critical response

Ostensibly, Scrooge rejects relationships with others because he seeks solitude and to only 'edge along the crowded paths of life', however, the complexity of Scrooge's character is that he is unable to establish and nurture relationships with others because everything he does is ultimately motivated by fear. He is afraid of poverty, rejection, and loss, and this acute fear outweighs his desire to connect. Dickens warns us against these fears and allowing them to take hold of us: if they do, we become 'solitary' and 'sharp', when instead life is about how we can help others and be a part of humankind.

Scrooge's early interactions with Fred and Bob may not be openly motivated by fear, but it is a subtle undercurrent to the way he interacts with them. His relationship with Bob is purely financial and so when Scrooge questions Bob needing time over Christmas, he comes back to the money he loses, saying that it is 'picking a man's pocket' by having time off over Christmas. This financial metaphor is indicative of Scrooge's fear – he views Bob wanting time off as a personal attack akin to having something stolen from his pocket as if Bob is intentionally taking his money from him. This fear of poverty is reflected in all of Scrooge's interactions, including when he threatens Bob that he will 'lose' his 'situation' – effectively telling us that Scrooge's relationship with Bob is only motivated by the money he can make from him, which is also shown in how he is overworked and underpaid. Scrooge's reactions to Fred, his antithesis, are also motivated by fear. His anger at Fred comes from Fred's love of Christmas (whilst acknowledging that he doesn't make money from it) in comparison to Scrooge's hatred. Significantly, when Scrooge lists all the various flaws of Christmas, all of them are financially motivated, with the paradoxical phrases of

---

How has the candidate successfully narrowed the question here to give themselves a thread to focus on?

This paragraph begins confidently and the candidate seeks to justify how the narrative fits into their argument, even if it is not obvious. This is a successful and critical way to begin.

How has this response ensured full coverage of the extract in this paragraph? Why is this particularly successful? What does it allow them to do in the rest of the essay?

'paying bills without money' and 'a year older, but not an hour richer', and these all stem from his fear of poverty, and so his broken relationship with his Fred is not necessarily a choice but instead necessary if Fred wants an uncle who will celebrate Christmas. It is easy to proclaim that Dickens encourages the reader to dislike the Scrooge of stave one, but if we unpick how his fears break down his relationships, we might consider ourselves sympathetic and want to truly understand where these fears originate.

Crucially, Scrooge's fear of poverty leads to a lack of interaction or relationship with the poor, both directly with Bob, and indirectly with those beyond his immediate interactions. Much like understanding Scrooge's complex character is difficult, understanding how he views the poor is more complex than a simple hatred for those in penury. Instead, Scrooge is ignorant of the plight of the poor (despite what seems a less than ideal upbringing himself) and this ignorance only fuels his fear. He views the poor as 'surplus' to society, as 'idle' people who deserve 'nothing', but only because he chooses to remain within the 'narrow limits' of his business. He perhaps says this perhaps due to a lack of understanding, but also because of his own fear: if he gives too much to the poor, then he will not have enough, and this motivates Scrooge's relationship with the wider society. When he questions 'are there no prisons?', he is motivated by fear because he knows if there are no other establishments then he will be expected to offer more. Interestingly, his use of questions here could be seen as a state of unease, checking that the 'workhouses' and 'Treadmill' still exist validates not only Scrooge's decision not to give to charity but also his own desire not to be one of the 'surplus' who deserves to reside in these places. Perhaps in many ways, Dickens is not only criticising those like Scrooge but also the Victorian government who force people into two states: fear because they have nothing or fear of having nothing. The change must start with those in poverty because, if their lives are better, perhaps those in a situation of privilege will not want such tight control on what they do have.

Scrooge's fears are extremely evident when we see his interactions with his former self and his reactions to the relationships he has had in the past. Scrooge clearly has love and affection for the individuals in his past (such as Fan, Fezziwig and Belle), and so we must be careful when we claim that Scrooge enjoys isolation and is merely apanthropic. He relishes the moments where he sees the people of his past – but, all of these people have been lost to Scrooge. We can, therefore, consider whether his lack of relationships in the present is a fear of loss rather than a dislike of human interaction. If we consider the interactions with Belle, his loss of Belle was directly related to his fear of poverty. She tells him: 'you fear the world too much' and then tells him that his aspirations have been destroyed by the 'master-passion, Gain'. This metaphor of Scrooge being almost in love with financial gain is often attributed to greed, but perhaps we might consider Belle's simple assertion of 'fear' being the motivation, rather

> The candidate continues their overall thread here, by focusing on the key ideas of fear and Scrooge being a complex character. It is clear that this is a well thought-out and coherent response.

> **How is this question carefully picked in order to support the overall argument? How does the candidate pull the evidence together?**

> The answer takes a wider approach to the consideration of authorial intent here.

> **How does the candidate use these thoughts to reach a point where they can justify their overall ideas?**

The analysis is seamlessly integrated into the response in this paragraph. It feels as if the candidate is exploring the text and their own interpretation, rather than listing ideas.

than something as simplistic as innate greed. When Scrooge sees Belle with her family and realises what he could have had, his mind must consider whether the financial implications of a family would outweigh his acute fear of being poor. In many ways, Scrooge is only dealing with extremes here: either he has more money than is necessary or he is in a state of suffering, so he hordes wealth and this leads to his rejection of relationships. As Belle says, he 'weigh[s] everything by Gain', and so ultimately, this costs him all human connections, much like the growing middle class in Victorian times, who pursued wealth only to the detriment of those in poverty.

Look at the evidence used in this paragraph – how are quotations used successfully here?

This argument was built on Scrooge being afraid and the candidate now explains that this fear is towards death rather than poverty by the end of the novella – a clever way of finalising the initial overall argument.

Ultimately, Scrooge changes his direction and chooses to 'gain' love and friendship rather than monetary wealth. Perhaps this decision is made when, in stave four, Scrooge is exposed to the reality of fearing poverty: it only leads to a lonely death, and you can't take the money with you. This fear of a 'neglected' grave, and his possessions being sold off, soon becomes a more substantial fear than that of poverty. The Ghost of Christmas Past reminds Scrooge, when seeing Fezziwig's party, that it is a small amount of Scrooge's 'mortal money' – in other words, Scrooge has plenty to spare, and it is the combination of all three ghosts, and what Scrooge learns about his own innate and complex fears, which result in Scrooge becoming Tim's 'second father'. This metaphor of Scrooge as Tim's 'father' is interesting, as Bob is also Tim's 'father', but this is not due to the sharing of wealth. It is instead founded on unconditional love and support, and placing your child above all other priorities, and so, as Scrooge's fear shifts away from poverty and loss, and instead to a fear of dying alone, he can channel this fear into something good: love and compassion for others. And we know it is not only the Cratchits that Scrooge builds these relationships with, it is also the wider community, as Scrooge gives the charity collectors a 'great many back payments', indicating he no longer fears poverty, as he is willing to hand over years of charitable contributions. By the end of the novella, Scrooge is 'as light as a feather', and perhaps this simile merely indicates he is no longer afraid – he will choose love and friendship over wealth. Dickens shows his readership that, in doing so, Scrooge not only lives a better existence but so do those around him, and this is the potential for change we all have if we let love conquer fear.

Critical response
This response is an excellent example of forming a clear line of argument and then ensuring each paragraph builds on this approach to the text. Put simply, this essay argues that Scrooge rejects others because of a fear of being poor. By working through the text in order, the candidate seeks to prove this fear across key moments in the text, with expertly integrated quotations and interwoven analysis. It is a critical response as it considers the less obvious interpretations at points, always supported by judicious and precise references.

The importance of the ghosts

2.3 Starting with this extract, explore how Dickens presents the importance of the ghosts within *A Christmas Carol.*

In this extract from stave four, Scrooge meets the Ghost of Christmas Yet to Come for the first time. He reacts to the ghost and they begin their journey.

Although well used to ghostly company by this time, Scrooge feared the silent shape so much that his legs trembled beneath him, and he found that he could hardly stand when he prepared to follow it. The Spirit paused a moment, as observing his condition, and giving him time to recover.

But Scrooge was all the worse for this. It thrilled him with a vague uncertain horror, to know that behind the dusky shroud, there were ghostly eyes intently fixed upon him, while he, though he stretched his own to the utmost, could see nothing but a spectral hand and one great heap of black.

'Ghost of the Future!' he exclaimed, 'I fear you more than any spectre I have seen. But as I know your purpose is to do me good, and as I hope to live to be another man from what I was, I am prepared to bear you company, and do it with a thankful heart. Will you not speak to me?'

It gave him no reply. The hand was pointed straight before them.

'Lead on!' said Scrooge. 'Lead on! The night is waning fast, and it is precious time to me, I know. Lead on, Spirit!'

The Phantom moved away as it had come towards him. Scrooge followed in the shadow of its dress, which bore him up, he thought, and carried him along.

Jacob Marley	Emotional connection – has to use the ghosts and the idea of the supernatural to suggest to readers that Scrooge may be close to death so he can cross over into the supernatural world to connect with the change he needs to make. Not just physically ill, but also emotionally and morally damaged. Has to be a frightening, horrific image of his past to shock Scrooge into realisation that his warnings matter. Significant that Dickens chooses the one character who we believe Scrooge has some kind of connection with.
Past	Ethereal, nebulous figure to help Scrooge to gently reconnect with his past. Some tender moments – sparks an initial emotion reaction within Scrooge, yet there is still a distinct lack of belief. Image of abundance with Fezziwig; contrast to the employer that Scrooge is.

Present	Dionysus – power to stand in the way of those who threaten to not embrace the spirit of Christmas. Shows the potential joy that he could share in, yet there is also a darker side. 'empty scabbard' and then Ignorance and Want. Scrooge's words horrify as he turns his back on his malthusian principles of previous.
Future	Extract: Darkness and fear – fear of the ghost = fear of the future – specifically his future. The realisation that change is imminent for both readers and Scrooge. The ghost does not need to speak – Scrooge will make his own messages and take his own answers.

2.3.1 Critical response

As with so many of the characters that inhabit Dickens' allegorical novella, the ghosts within *A Christmas Carol* are employed by him as vehicles to both educate and transform Scrooge and his outlook. This is the change that Dickens wished to see both within Scrooge and the wealthy of Victorian society as a whole and, as such, the ghosts are potentially one of the most important character devices within the whole novella as this overriding aim is achieved primarily as a result of their interventions.

Whilst considering the importance of the ghosts and their roles, it is incredibly significant to acknowledge that it is the supernatural element of the novella that allows for this course of interventions to occur. It is widely believed that Scrooge takes a 'little saucepan of gruel' for his dinner but this is an incorrect assumption. We are told previously that Scrooge ate his 'melancholy dinner' in a 'melancholy tavern', but this appears to be overlooked as many readers believe that Scrooge eats his small bowl of 'gruel' due to his 'tight-fisted' nature. Yet, upon closer inspection, we see that Dickens signposts us to the fact that 'Scrooge had a cold in his head'. We have learned that Scrooge has been in his current mindset for the years since Marley has died, so the question as to why is it at this very point that the ghosts stage an intervention for him may be asked at this point. Marley's ghost appears to answer the question that curious readers, and Scrooge himself, have regarding this appearance, acknowledging it with 'How it is that I appear before you in a shape that you can see' with the response that '[he] may not tell', before proceeding to explain to Scrooge that he has 'sat invisible beside [him] many and many a day'. This could suggest to us that Scrooge does not just have a 'cold in his head', but that he is actually incredibly close to passing into the world that the ghosts inhabit forever. It could be suggested that the ghosts of the novella offer Scrooge one last chance through these encounters to show that he is indeed 'worthy' of life within the 'mortal' world. Whilst the novella was designed to 'haunt [...] houses pleasantly', the idea of an 'invisible' judge sitting beside readers may have links to an omnipotent Christian God who watches over them throughout the year. At the most significant time of the year within the Christian calendar, this may serve

---

How does the candidate make it clear that this novel has a purpose and that the characters are just that?

The candidate's confidence with the text is clear immediately. They address the nuances of the text in order to support their argument.

The sustained and careful development of ideas here shows the candidate's thoughtful engagement with the text.

How does the candidate's treatment of the context here support their ideas?

as a stark reminder that readers should attempt to embody Christian morals and values all year round and that this novella provides them with one last chance to do so and re-align themselves just as the ghosts help Scrooge to do.

The ghost of Jacob Marley appears to Scrooge in stave one in a frightening guise. Scrooge recognises Marley, which is something that marks Marley as a different kind of ghost within the novella. It is significant that Dickens ensures that the first ghost that Scrooge encounters is one with whom he had an emotional connection on Earth. Marley becomes synonymous with the image of chains within this stave and much mention is made of them as Dickens describes Marley as letting out a 'frightful cry' and shaking 'its chain with such a dismal and appalling noise'. Not only do the chains suggest the imprisonment that awaits Scrooge should he fail to correct his behaviour and recognise the error of his ways, but they also allow for Scrooge to recognise that it is not just the poor who can be viewed as criminals who need to be incarcerated. It is also significant here that Dickens dehumanises Marley, describing him as a 'spirit' who shakes 'its chain'. Dickens chooses to present Scrooge with a familiar figure and one who he clearly held affection for as we know that he 'never rubbed out old Marley's name', this subtle modulation in language from 'his' to 'its' could suggest that it does not matter who these messages come from. It matters that the messages are listened to and acknowledged.

Ostensibly, the three ghosts that follow Jacob Marley's appearance are similar to one another in that they are unknown figures who will allow Scrooge a 'hope and chance of escaping [Marley's] fate', but this is where the similarity ends. The ghosts all serve very different purposes and their methods and messages differ depending on Scrooge's reaction both to them and the previous ghost. Scrooge is clearly fearful of the first spirit's visit so much so that the 'curtains of his bed were drawn aside' by 'a hand' that was not his own. This not only shows that Scrooge is reluctant to meet the ghost but also that it symbolises his greater reluctance to engage with its messages. As such, Dickens' Ghost of Christmas Past is an ethereal and nebulous figure that allows him to gently reconnect with his past. There are some tender moments within this stave as Scrooge declares that he 'should like to be able to say a word or two to my clerk just now' where he subtly acknowledges the differences between himself and Fezziwig, yet there is no definitive change established within Scrooge. Scrooge's use of imperatives at the end of the stave to 'Leave me! Take me back. Haunt me no longer' suggest that Scrooge still believes that he can control the spirits and not that they must be allowed to control his outlook. Scrooge's cry for the spirit to 'haunt [him] no longer' reinforces Scrooge's belief that this supernatural interaction is fleeting and can stop at any time. Scrooge does not yet realise that the only way in which he escapes such 'shadows' is if he actively changes his behaviour and not just his thoughts.

> **Has the candidate fully explained why Marley is different to the other ghosts here? Do they need to?**

> Whilst this is a response about the ghosts, the candidate also refers to other key themes within the novel to support their ideas.

> **How could the candidate ensure that their writing stays analytical over narrative?**

> The candidate's use of precise and varied references show a deep engagement with the text.

Can you identify the tentative language with which this candidate poses suggestions about the text here?

Whilst the candidate makes suggestions about key textual ideas here, they also link this to their developed understanding of the context. This enhances their response and gives it real depth.

Why is it important that the candidate keeps returning to the writer's intentions?

The candidate has good coverage of the text here and uses a wide range of evidence from across the novel.

The ability to understand more than the literal meanings of parts of the text sustains this critical response.

Just as Scrooge's internal darkness refuses to lift, Dickens presents Scrooge with a ghost who appears to be abundant and prosperous – being described as a 'jolly giant' by Dickens – yet, there is a darker undertone to this third ghost that lurks beneath the ghost's robes. The ghost is described positively by Dickens with 'its genial face, its sparkling eye, its open hand, its cheery voice, its unconstrained demeanour, and its joyful air.' The plethora of positive adjectives through the listing here could be seen to represent the physical changes also needed within Scrooge, yet this abundantly positive description is followed by the acknowledgement that 'girded round its middle was an antique scabbard; but no sword was in it'. What this secondary description could suggest to us is that whilst the ghost is outwardly positive, it also has previously held a 'sword' that could suggest that it is not afraid to harm those who refute its ideas. As Scrooge walks with the ghost, he would have been aware of the gargantuan size of the 'jolly giant' and note the messages that he presents. The significance of the Ghost of Christmas Present's physical size, therefore, may be used to frighten and shock Scrooge into listening to his messages. The prompting of an emotional response previously has not triggered any definitive actions thus leaving Dickens to employ a ghost who must take a different approach to engineering change. Specifically, within this stave, a reader is presented with many images of suffering as it was believed by followers of Malthus that poverty was indeed humanity's inescapable fate if they had not the means to provide for themselves and their families. This image would most likely jar with modern readers and it is at this point that Scrooge also appears to abandon his Malthusian views of the past. Asking the spirit to 'tell [him] if Tiny Tim shall live' and questioning whether there is 'refuge or resource' for the manifestations of the industrial poor in Ignorance and Want, Dickens begins to highlight that if a man of Scrooge's fixed views can change his outlook then so could others who find themselves of Scrooge's ilk outside of the fictional world. The Spirit's importance within this stave is in his ability to rally against everything that Scrooge – and, therefore, Malthusian followers – would have believed in. Scrooge's concern for the figures of Ignorance and Want at the end of this stave shows his increasing capacity for change and Dickens' description of them as being 'meagre, ragged, scowling, wolfish' highlights the lessons that these children have come to show him. Specifically, the adjective 'wolfish' demonstrates the difficult and unpalatable lesson that Scrooge must swallow in order to live in the 'past, present and future'. It was often believed that wolves were symbolic of the teaching of difficult lessons within Eastern European literature and it is doubtful that Dickens would have overlooked this.

Scrooge's 'thankful heart' is exposed within stave four, which almost immediately signifies his transformation from object to person with the one defining difference between an object such as 'flint' or an 'oyster' being its capacity for love, which is so often symbolised through the organ of the heart. Significantly, the ghost in stave four does not teach Scrooge anything that is different to the previous ghosts of the novella. Instead, Scrooge is able to express what he has learnt and recognise the requirement for him to have physically and emotionally changed. We are told that Scrooge 'feared the silent shape' and Scrooge himself exclaims that 'Spectre, I fear you more than any spectre I have seen', with the repetition of the conjugations of the verb 'fear' signposting the reader to the fact that it is not necessarily the figure that the ghost fears, but more what it represents – in this case, the future. Scrooge cannot bear to live in the future that he has created for himself, pleading with the spirit to 'tell me I may sponge away the writing on this stone' where the sheer desperation for him to change is conveyed through the painstaking verb 'sponge'. This acknowledges that Scrooge cannot change everything immediately, but much like cleaning with a 'sponge', he will need to mop up his errors bit by bit before the 'stone' is clear again.

How does dealing with short quotations support the overall response here?

It is without a doubt that the ghosts within *A Christmas Carol* are imperative to the transformation that Scrooge undergoes. Similar to a process of reincarnation, Scrooge acknowledges within stave five that he is 'quite a baby' again where he is an unblemished version of himself, unshackled from the misgivings of his path as he strives to live in the 'present' as a 'second father' to Tiny Tim. It is the ghosts that provide him with the 'springtime in the haggard winter of his life' as, without them, it could be believed that his fate would have been an incredibly different one. It is the ghosts that allow for Dickens to deliver his message that if Scrooge can change, anyone can within his 'ghostly little book'.

The closing tone here is convincing and confident. The candidate refers to points raised earlier and rounds off their argument. This is a comprehensive and cohesive finish.

Critical response

This response is assured and perceptive throughout. The style of writing exudes confidence and it is clear that the candidate has absolute textual security. There is a wide range of references used; some are used to develop analysis and others are used as drop quotations to enhance the confident and personal style of writing. There is extensive exploration of contextual factors that help to explore the writer's overall intentions. This essay stays focused and purposeful throughout. The writing is controlled and impressive.

Social responsibility

2.4 Starting with this extract, explore how Dickens highlights the importance of social responsibility in *A Christmas Carol*.

In this extract from stave two, the Ghost of Christmas Past takes Scrooge to see his former boss, Fezziwig. At the end of the night, he discusses what he has seen with the ghost.

During the whole of this time, Scrooge had acted like a man out of his wits. His heart and soul were in the scene, and with his former self. He corroborated everything, remembered everything, enjoyed everything, and underwent the strangest agitation. It was not until now, when the bright faces of his former self and Dick were turned from them, that he remembered the Ghost, and became conscious that it was looking full upon him, while the light upon its head burnt very clear.

'A small matter,' said the Ghost, 'to make these silly folks so full of gratitude.'

'Small!' echoed Scrooge.

The Spirit signed to him to listen to the two apprentices, who were pouring out their hearts in praise of Fezziwig: and when he had done so, said,

'Why! Is it not? He has spent but a few pounds of your mortal money: three or four perhaps. Is that so much that he deserves this praise?'

'It isn't that,' said Scrooge, heated by the remark, and speaking unconsciously like his former, not his latter, self. 'It isn't that, Spirit. He has the power to render us happy or unhappy; to make our service light or burdensome; a pleasure or a toil. Say that his power lies in words and looks; in things so slight and insignificant that it is impossible to add and count 'em up: what then? The happiness he gives, is quite as great as if it cost a fortune.'

He felt the Spirit's glance, and stopped.

'What is the matter?' asked the Ghost.

'Nothing particular,' said Scrooge.

'Something, I think?' the Ghost insisted.

'No,' said Scrooge, 'No. I should like to be able to say a word or two to my clerk just now. That's all.'

2.4.1 Critical response

At a time where policymakers and the ruling classes felt that poverty was being perpetuated by the provision of poor law relief, it could be suggested that it is little wonder that Scrooge presents in the way he does at the opening of the novella. Reacting to the condition of society in 1843, Dickens attempts to highlight the real need for individuals to take responsibility for others and to fulfil their civic duty. Dickens achieves this through characters who show the clear benefits that come to fruition when one takes their social responsibility seriously.

Dickens' employment of many a character within the novella who attempt to highlight the importance of social responsibility to Scrooge begins with the appearance of the ghost of Jacob Marley. Despite Scrooge believing that he will find Marley to 'speak comfort' to him, he believes that essentially Marley will condone his approach to his business. Marley retorts that 'Mankind was my business. The common welfare was my business; charity, mercy, forbearance, and benevolence, were, all, my business. ' Through allowing Scrooge to see that even 'a good man of business' such as Marley now acknowledges that business is not just to be associated with the process of profiting financially allows Scrooge to understand that it is indeed his 'business' to support 'Mankind'. Marley's listing allows for Scrooge to understand what social responsibility looked like to Dickens in that it is to do with 'charity' and 'benevolence', yet at this point in the novella, it is clear that Scrooge is not able to recognise these behaviours and 'business' in his own daily existence.

In opposition to Marley's listing of the characteristics of social responsibility, Scrooge himself is described as a 'squeezing, wrenching, grasping, scraping, clutching, covetous, old sinner' highlighting to a reader the differences in what Marley knows he should have been in comparison to what Scrooge currently is. The adjective 'covetous' is important here as it suggests that Scrooge is not only interested in keeping things to himself, but that he also desires what others have. Yet, ironically, that is the very thing he dislikes in others, most notably in the poor, as this behaviour is exhibited when the charity collectors visit Scrooge in stave one. Questioning 'Are there no prisons? ' and whether 'the Union workhouses [...] are [...] still in operation?', Scrooge's use of the supercilious rhetorical questions is not only suggestive of his avaricious nature, but they also display a sense of arrogance that could lead us to believe that Scrooge has forgotten just how difficult it is to be poor. After all, we are well aware that Scrooge was not always the 'man of business' that he is in stave one, and Dickens purposefully shows us that he felt that 'there is nothing on which [the world] is so hard as poverty, and there is nothing it professes to condemn with such severity as the pursuit of wealth!' in stave two. It could be suggested that Scrooge has, in fact, not forgotten the struggles of a life fuelled by poverty, but moreover that he is so acutely aware of it that his fears of a life lived in poverty are made manifest through his misanthropic behaviours. Through his fear, Scrooge shuns

A critical tone is established from the opening. The candidate confidently presents contextual ideas to sit their argument against.

How does the candidate ensure that all of their writing is focused on the set task?

Judicious references are used to highlight central ideas.

The candidate shows their confidence with the text as they link ideas from across the novel to highlight their ideas.

the opportunities to support others and so, in order for Dickens to show that one could both carve out a generous living for oneself alongside supporting others in society who were potentially less fortunate, he presents him with the character of Fezziwig.

Fezziwig is an interesting character within the novella as he is clearly a capitalist yet is not carved from the same mercenary cloth as Scrooge. Fezziwig has the means to lay on a lavish and bountiful party on Christmas Eve, which highlights his success within business as he can afford to do such a thing, yet Scrooge acknowledges that 'The happiness he gives, is quite as great as if it cost a fortune.' At this point, the juxtaposing language of 'happiness' and 'fortune' suggests that Scrooge has not quite understood that money and financial gain are not the sole markers of happiness. Scrooge does, however, recognise the value of Fezziwig's generosity in that he uses the noun 'fortune' to describe the amount of pleasure that he gives. This use of financial lexicon indicates that this is the only way in which Scrooge currently knows how to describe and measure something of immense value. Within this short scene, Scrooge is only an apprentice, yet the memories and the 'light' that is associated with this extract supports Dickens in highlighting the positive power of generosity and supporting others around you. This message is transformational even if it only allows Scrooge to want 'to be able to say a word or two to my clerk just now', as a 'word' is more than Scrooge has been obliged to give Bob Cratchit in the past.

As an allegorical novella, Dickens knows that what has happened in the past cannot be changed and that lessons must be learned from it in order to pave the way for a brighter and more socially inclusive future. No stranger to the harsh reality of a life lived in poverty, Dickens would have keenly felt the implications of the New Poor Law Amendment Act of 1834, which laid the blame for poverty and unemployment upon 'idle people' and their actions. Despite there being charitable and philanthropic organisations at work within Victorian Britain, characters such as Scrooge outside of Dickens' fictitious world would have been able to avoid the reality of lives lived in poverty, should they have wanted to, as the teachings of Malthus almost helped to reassure them that the poor were 'wretched' creatures who were nothing more than the 'surplus population'. In order to look to the future, Dickens uses characters of children as a device to warn Scrooge and wider readers of the dangers of a society that fails to take social responsibility for its future. Within stave three, we are introduced to the character of Tiny Tim who would be nothing more than a 'crutch without an owner' if the 'shadows' of the future were not changed. Dickens shows us that should Scrooge fail to protect Tiny Tim, and all those children in poverty whom he also represents, then he also fails in his own social responsibility.

The image of children is again used by Dickens through the presentation of the children of Ignorance and Want. Drawn 'from the foldings of [the ghost's] robe', these children metaphorically represent the hidden truth of poverty; the industrial poor who had been forgotten by society. As the ghost tells Scrooge that 'They are Man's', Dickens allows readers to understand that these children are the 'business' and responsibility of society. These children, representing the 'Ignorance' and 'Want' that society should 'beware' in the future will not fail to exist, but these social problems will no longer be concealed from view and will instead produce a society with 'Doom' written all over it as children are the future of any society in the years to come. Scrooge's modulation of language at the close of this stave from 'Are there no prisons?' to 'Have they no refuge or resource?' depicts the changing attitudes that Dickens so desperately needed society to behold. Gone is the punitive and vengeful tone of stave one and in its place, we see a much more concerned and socialist tone, suggesting that society will only be able to fulfil its civic duty if it is shown the 'wretched' and 'abject' reality of its poorest.

A more promising and palatable future is displayed within stave five as Scrooge allows for the people he once felt were 'idle' to become 'merry', raising Bob's salary and becoming a 'second father to Tiny Tim'. Notably, Dickens uses the image of father and son to show the transformation of Scrooge to a reader, which could suggest that society needs, as a whole, to act as a father to its children and future. Dickens' long-ranging aim for society to take greater social responsibility was not realised until much later outside of his political diatribe, however, it was not until the Beveridge Report was published in 1942 that welfare from the cradle to the grave was made a reality within Britain. The comprehensive system of welfare support that is appreciated in modern society now provides the 'refuge' and 'resource' that Dickens so longed for Tiny Tim to be blessed by.

> Mature and sophisticated vocabulary choices elevate the written style.

> **Can you recognise the micro to macro ideas presented to conclude cohesively?**

Critical response

This response pays great attention to the important and influential context of the novella which allows the candidate to really develop their ideas convincingly with context at the heart of their argument. The candidate shows their appreciation of how Dickens achieves specific effects through his language use and presentation of ideas. This keeps the focus of the writer's intentions at the forefront of the reader's mind and ensures that the essay fully responds to the set question. References are drawn from across the novel showing good textual security and a sophisticated awareness of how ideas link together and support one another.

The Cratchit family

2.5 Starting with this extract, explore how Dickens presents the Cratchit family in *A Christmas Carol.*

In this extract from stave four Scrooge, the Ghost of Christmas Yet to Come visits the Cratchit family. Bob arrives home and they discuss the loss of their son, Tiny Tim.

They were very quiet again. At last she said, and in a steady, cheerful voice, that only faltered once:

'I have known him walk with—I have known him walk with Tiny Tim upon his shoulder, very fast indeed.'

'And so have I,' cried Peter. 'Often.'

'And so have I,' exclaimed another. So had all.

'But he was very light to carry,' she resumed, intent upon her work, 'and his father loved him so, that it was no trouble: no trouble. And there is your father at the door!'

She hurried out to meet him; and little Bob in his comforter—he had need of it, poor fellow—came in. His tea was ready for him on the hob, and they all tried who should help him to it most. Then the two young Cratchits got upon his knees and laid, each child a little cheek, against his face, as if they said, 'Don't mind it, father. Don't be grieved!'

Bob was very cheerful with them, and spoke pleasantly to all the family. He looked at the work upon the table, and praised the industry and speed of Mrs. Cratchit and the girls. They would be done long before Sunday, he said.

'Sunday! You went to-day, then, Robert?' said his wife.

'Yes, my dear,' returned Bob. 'I wish you could have gone. It would have done you good to see how green a place it is. But you'll see it often. I promised him that I would walk there on a Sunday. My little, little child!' cried Bob. 'My little child!'

He broke down all at once. He couldn't help it. If he could have helped it, he and his child would have been farther apart perhaps than they were.

He left the room, and went up-stairs into the room above, which was lighted cheerfully, and hung with Christmas. There was a chair set close beside the child, and there were signs of some one having been there, lately. Poor Bob sat down in it, and when he had thought a little and composed himself, he kissed the little face. He was reconciled to what had happened, and went down again quite happy.

They drew about the fire, and talked; the girls and mother working still.

2.5.1 Critical response

Cratchits used overall to symbolise both the warmth and resilience of the poor (juxtaposed with Scrooge's ignorance of this and lack of warmth). Their treatment is highlighted because both reader and Scrooge are ignorant.	
'Brave in ribbons' 'eked out' 'small pudding for a large family'	Family shown as resilient; despite difficulties, they work to ensure they share. Juxtaposition: thankful/grateful despite having little.
'Walk [...] very fast indeed' 'Tim's blood horse'	Strength highlighted, TT is not a burden. Scrooge ignorant to the struggles.
'About the fire' ('frosty rime') 'green a place'	Warmth associated with family (unlike Scrooge) and how TT's death is treated with respect and dignity.
'Second father' 'assist your struggling family' 'raise your wages'	Scrooge no longer ignorant (like reader) = now respects resilience and understands struggles, so willing to support family.

Having spent some time as a child in a blacking factory and being acutely aware of the plight of the poor, Dickens methodically destroys the ignorance and disgust that many of his middle- and upper-class readers would have held against the lower classes of Victorian Britain. Warm, brave and far from 'idle', the Cratchits represent the strength of the poor, starkly juxtaposed with the ignorance and cold of the rich. Dickens utilises the Cratchit family as a symbol of the resilience of the poor, not only to ensure Scrooge is aware of what he misunderstands but also to engage his Victorian readership in the truth of those who exist on the breadline.

Our first real understanding of the Cratchit family comes in the lively and loving scene of stave three, where the family are resilient despite the difficulties they must face. There is a real sense of camaraderie amongst the family, who each have their role within the family home, and no one rests or resists contributing (unlike the assertion of Scrooge in stave one that the poor are 'idle'). Dickens begins to deconstruct Scrooge's (and the reader's) ignorance, as the poor do not weep and moan about their lot in life, but instead remain 'brave in ribbons', a metaphor used to illustrate that they make do with what they have and will use cheap items to ensure that Christmas is still a special day. When the family eat their meal, Dickens' use of the verb 'eked' establishes the resourceful aspect of the Cratchits; they are frugal and careful and ensure that everyone has enough to eat by attention to how they make their food and how they distribute it. This is not the family Scrooge had expected. Significantly, the family are not desperate or dependent on others but instead are grateful for what they have, and are filled with the love they have for each other rather than monetary gain (again, juxtaposed with Scrooge's earlier behaviour). When we are informed that no one would have considered it 'a small pudding for a large family', the simple juxtaposition of 'small' and 'large' highlights that the family are not

> How does this introduction show an awareness of the text as a construct? How does it swiftly embed context into the overall response?

> The response is immediately exploratory and convincing. Articulate phrasing of ideas is supported by excellent knowledge of the text.

> In what ways does the candidate show fine-grained and specific analysis throughout this paragraph?

This is clearly a well-structured argument. The candidate constantly returns to the key words used in their introduction.

Why do you think the candidate has chosen not to jump straight into analysing the extract? Why does the analysis of the extract work better following this explanation?

This candidate makes specific and detailed links between the context (mainly social and historical) to the task, ensuring they consider reader impact and writer's message alongside their own interpretation.

How is ambitious vocabulary used successfully in the opening sentences of this paragraph?

Throughout this part of the paragraph the candidate uses precise and judicious quotation choice to build their argument. Each reference is embedded within the response in an academic way, allowing the answer to feel critical and sophisticated.

ignorant – they are aware that they do not have much – but instead are grateful and not rude enough to suggest that their dinner is lacking. This scene is key in establishing the reality of the poor and Dickens forces Scrooge and his Victorian readership to be exposed to the reality of the poor: they are grateful, resourceful and resilient, far from the 'idle' individuals he (and probably the reader) expects.

The role of Tiny Tim within the Cratchit family is key not only in understanding their attitude to life but also in ensuring Scrooge's understanding of the family shifts. From Scrooge's perspective, Tiny Tim must indicate a financial burden on the family. Dickens draws our attention to Scrooge's wariness of the financial implications of a family when he says to the ghost that 1800 brothers must be a 'tremendous family to provide for'. For the Cratchits however, Tiny Tim is never a burden and the reader finds themselves hoping for his survival, much like Scrooge, as we watch the frail and brave child reflect on what he sees at Christmas. Dickens shows both the reader and Scrooge that Tiny Tim is never a burden by reversing our expectations of his impact on the family. We learn that Bob would 'walk [...] very fast indeed' when carrying Tiny Tim and that Bob had become his 'blood-horse'. Metaphorically, Dickens is indicating that, far from being extra weight to carry, Tim actually improves Bob physically, and so the reward of having him in the Cratchit family outweighs any kind of physical or financial burden he creates. This, of course, is hard for Scrooge to understand – as Belle tells him, Scrooge 'weigh[s] everything by Gain' and so he must see Tim and the influence he has on the family to understand why it's important for him to survive. The physical and emotional strength of the poor is highlighted here, and Scrooge cannot help but wish to know if 'Tiny Tim will live' – the same emotional reaction Dickens wants of his reader. Whilst the rich remain ignorant to the Cratchits' struggles, it is easy to treat them as 'surplus population' – it is only once they know the reality of the poor's strength and struggles that they (Scrooge and the reader) will try and do something in the wider society to actively prevent these difficulties.

The Cratchit family's bleak and tragic future is pivotal in destroying Scrooge's ignorance towards the poor and helping him to understand what will matter in death. In stave four, Dickens cleverly engineers a blatant juxtaposition between the death of Scrooge and the death of Tiny Tim to make a clear (if brutal) message: how you treat people in life will be how you are treated in death. Tim's caring and compassionate treatment of others is reflected in the mourning of the Cratchit family, and how much attention and care they pay to lay him to rest. The room where Tim is 'lighted cheerfully' and, evidently, regularly visited, and the family gather 'about the fire' after talking about how 'green' the place is where Tim will be buried. The motif of warmth is used throughout to link to the Cratchit family, from the busy scene in stave three to the mourning scene in stave four, we still get a sense of warmth in the family as they do everything together; their warmth unites them and is linked to their kindness. This juxtaposes the motif of cold linked to Scrooge, with his 'frosty rime' in the opening of the novella, and his empty house, with death described as 'cold, cold'. Scrooge's cold is associated with his bitter and distant relationships with others (juxtaposing the Cratchits) and this is continued into the descriptions of Tim's and Scrooge's deaths. Whilst Tim's resting place is a 'green' place that will be seen 'often', Scrooge's graveyard is 'neglected' and 'choked' with 'weeds'. So despite the lack of wealth that Tiny Tim had in life, his death is surrounded by a wealth of mourning and warmth, and he will be buried in a beautiful place. This harsh juxtaposition with Scrooge serves to, yet again, break down Scrooge's (and the reader's) ignorance. In these two deaths in stave four, Scrooge and the reader are forced to see what truly matters, family and strength rather than wealth and anger.

As the novella draws to a close, we realise that Scrooge is no longer ignorant and he is now able to support the Cratchits now that he understands them. When Scrooge commits to improving the Cratchits' lives, this is not a temporary resolve, but a desire to build a long-lasting connection with the family. When Scrooge commits to Bob that he will 'assist [his] struggling family', he shows not only a desire to make a change but also a genuine understanding of the family. They are 'struggling', but Scrooge understands that he is to blame for this. He agrees to 'raise' Bob's salary, but the impact he has is not only monetary, as he also becomes a 'second father' to Tiny Tim. Scrooge's final instruction to Bob is to 'make up the fires' and to buy another coal scuttle. This shows a drastic change to the 'one coal' that Bob is given at the start. This illustrates how the Cratchits' warmth and compassion has spread to Scrooge in stave five, who now understands not only the literal warmth that Bob needs in the workplace but also the metaphorical warmth offered by family that Scrooge needs himself. When Scrooge plans to 'discuss' the family's 'affairs' with Bob, he is not wanting to pry but, instead, Dickens is showing the absence of ignorance and a genuine desire to know more about the Cratchits' lives. So, in many ways, the Cratchits are a vehicle for Dickens to help Scrooge and the reader understand the poor, but they are also symbolic of hope: the hope that if we break down the ignorance of the rich, then we can begin to understand the poor; that they may struggle, but they are grateful and resourceful and their lives (and, indeed, deaths) matter far more than we realise.

> **How do the opening sentences here consider the structure of the novella?**

> **How is the overall argument still being proved at this point?**

> The candidate concludes by bringing together their overall argument alongside Dickens' intentions. It is a convincing and mature closing sentence.

Critical response

Whilst there are lots of ways to respond to the Cratchit family, the candidate here expertly covers a wide range of key moments in addressing this task. There is some fine-grained analysis alongside some structural consideration; they think about how Scrooge's attitude to the poor changes due to the way the Cratchits are presented. This task lends itself well to AO3, but here the candidate makes detailed and specific link between social context, the bigger concepts explored within A Christmas Carol, and Dickens' message and intentions.

The importance of settings

2.6 Starting with this extract, explore how Dickens presents the importance of the settings within *A Christmas Carol*.

In this extract from stave three, Scrooge and the Ghost of Christmas Present leave the Cratchits and journey through the streets of London. They then arrive at a deserted location.

By this time it was getting dark, and snowing pretty heavily; and as Scrooge and the Spirit went along the streets, the brightness of the roaring fires in kitchens, parlours, and all sorts of rooms, was wonderful. Here, the flickering of the blaze showed preparations for a cosy dinner, with hot plates baking through and through before the fire, and deep red curtains, ready to be drawn to shut out cold and darkness. There all the children of the house were running out into the snow to meet their married sisters, brothers, cousins, uncles, aunts, and be the first to greet them. Here, again, were shadows on the window-blind of guests assembling; and there a group of handsome girls, all hooded and fur-booted, and all chattering at once, tripped lightly off to some near neighbour's house; where, woe upon the single man who saw them enter—artful witches, well they knew it—in a glow!

But, if you had judged from the numbers of people on their way to friendly gatherings, you might have thought that no one was at home to give them welcome when they got there, instead of every house expecting company, and piling up its fires half-chimney high. Blessings on it, how the Ghost exulted! How it bared its breadth of breast, and opened its capacious palm, and floated on, outpouring, with a generous hand, its bright and harmless mirth on everything within its reach! The very lamplighter, who ran on before, dotting the dusky street with specks of light, and who was dressed to spend the evening somewhere, laughed out loudly as the Spirit passed, though little kenned the lamplighter that he had any company but Christmas!

And now, without a word of warning from the Ghost, they stood upon a bleak and desert moor, where monstrous masses of rude stone were cast about, as though it were the burial-place of giants; and water spread itself wheresoever it listed, or would have done so, but for the frost that held it prisoner; and nothing grew but moss and furze, and coarse rank grass. Down in the west the setting sun had left a streak of fiery red, which glared upon the desolation for an instant, like a sullen eye, and frowning lower, lower, lower yet, was lost in the thick gloom of darkest night.

2.6.1 Critical response

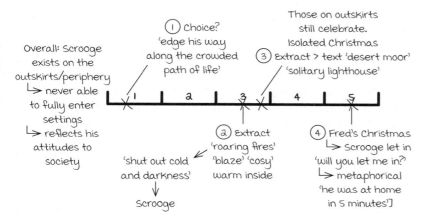

Existing predominantly on the outskirts of society, Scrooge begins the novel as someone who enjoys being on the 'edge' of life. In remaining on the periphery, however, Scrooge never fully engages with society or those around him and Dickens utilises settings to highlight this. The settings become a metaphor for Scrooge's engagement with the world and it is only at the novel's close – when Scrooge is ready to integrate himself into society – that he is no longer on the outskirts of the settings he visits. Dickens reinforces the moral message that life can only be enjoyed when you are a part of it, while life on the outskirts can be lonely.

Scrooge lives on the outskirts of society in stave one because he chooses to do so. We are told that Scrooge chooses to 'edge his way along the crowded path of life' – a complex metaphor that illustrates Scrooge's apanthropic existence. Scrooge's apanthropy, his love of solitude, ensures he never truly involves himself in any relationships but that he exists only on the periphery. The juxtaposition between 'edge' and 'crowded' draws a clear boundary between the usual existence of humanity and Scrooge's way of existing. Typically, humans crave contact and want to engage in the world around them but Scrooge is the opposite of this and, in the metaphorical 'path of life', he would rather not live his life, instead just move his way around life, ignoring others and his instinct for human connection. The verb 'edge' is indicative of Scrooge's behaviour throughout the novella: his ignorance is fuelled by his choice to 'edge' around things. He decided to 'edge' around his memories, ensuring that he does not suffer the pity for his younger self, the anger at his choices with Belle, or his love for Fan and Fezziwig. He also 'edges' around the poor and Fred in the present, and it

This is a confident and exploratory opening, which shows excellent textual security, as well as understanding the big ideas of the text.

This opening point signposts a well-structured argument, with a clear topic sentence used to begin this paragraph.

is the ghosts who attempt to force Scrooge into these memories, places, and relationships, but he still tries to remain on the outskirts of these settings. Each setting, therefore, becomes a metaphor for Scrooge's changing understanding and relationships with others, and this becomes symbolic of his attitude to life in general. Perhaps Dickens knows this is not just the life of Scrooge, but a life common to many in the Victorian era: a desire to 'edge' around life means to never fully engage with humanity, and this allows the many divides of Victorian England to grow and deepen.

There is extremely clever use of the extract here. By selecting short, judicious quotations, the candidate is able to use the extract as a justification of their overall argument.

Whilst many of the journeys with the ghosts serve to force Scrooge away from the outskirts, moments within his journey are used to highlight this divide. Significantly, in this extract, Scrooge and the Ghost of Christmas Present exist very literally on the outskirts of Christmas, and this walk through the streets of London is clearly indicative of Scrooge's relationship with the wider society. Dickens utilises the setting here to set up clear boundaries between Scrooge and the world around him: he is in the 'cold', those inside are 'cosy' with 'fires'; Scrooge is out in the 'darkness' whilst the rooms are lit with a 'blaze'. Scrooge is outside alone (except for the ghost) but inside 'guests', 'neighbours' and families meetings. Here, the path Scrooge chooses is no longer the 'edge' of life, but a clear division between happiness and loneliness. Scrooge may have previously chose solitude, but he does not realise what he is missing out on, and the metaphorically closed up houses with their warmth and Christmas cheer highlight to Scrooge exactly what he is missing out on. Dickens utilises this setting here to show that whilst Scrooge may choose the 'edge' of life, he only chooses to lack other things, such as warmth and love. The juxtaposition between what is inside (a semantic field of warmth highlights this: 'blaze' 'fires' and 'hot') and what is outside is far from subtle, as is the comment that the families 'shut out cold and darkness' – a blatant metaphor for Scrooge being 'shut out' from enjoying any of the events inside. The ghost, of course, is not part of this darkness, as he engages with the people inside through his torch and 'generous hand', so whilst he is physically outside, he is not existing on the periphery like Scrooge chooses to. Dickens utilises this key moment as a reminder to the reader of everything you can miss out on if you decide to live on the outskirts of life: the warmth, love, and cheer of genuine human connection are there, but you must make an effort to access it (and at this point, Scrooge is not willing to).

How does the candidate explore patterns of language in this paragraph? Why is this a successful way to analyse language?

How does the candidate constantly return to the task and overall argument?

A strong knowledge of the text is evident here. This is an unusual part to pick but the seven words remembered open up the candidate's response and allows them to critically explore the text. It is an excellent decision.

Scrooge believes that his self-imposed isolation forces him to not engage with others or the joy of Christmas, but the ghost soon shows Scrooge the error of this judgement. Settings are used by Dickens at this point to reflect the lives of isolated individuals who still feel the joy of human connection and Christmas cheer, despite existing quite literally on the outskirts of life. In the 'solitary lighthouse' and 'desert moor' Dickens shows Scrooge, and indeed the reader, the reality that living on the outskirts physically does not have to change your humanity. So Scrooge views these harsh and bleak settings, a metaphor perhaps for the way he lives his life, but then realises that the people within are not isolated or solitary, but instead still have 'fires' and still sing Christmas songs and celebrate Christmas time. And of course, with these people, the ghost continues to spread his Christmas cheer, because these people do not exist on the edge of life in the same way as Scrooge. Scrooge realises his choice at this moment, reflecting how it might be to exist in a 'lonely darkness', and at this point, we realise Scrooge's understanding of himself, and how he exists on the periphery, is now changing. At this moment, he hears a laugh and is taken to Fred's house – an interesting moment, where Scrooge is unable to be involved in the party, but for the first time, he actually wants to join in, and 'begged like a boy' to stay. At this point Scrooge's way of engaging with the world is changing: he wants to be a part of it, he does not want to only be on the 'edge' anymore, but instead by a part of the crowd. In many ways, these isolated settings are a catalyst for changing Scrooge's engagement with the world, and a key way Dickens uses settings to offer a message on how we should live our lives.

How does this response build a well-structured argument? Are there simple things they do which can be replicated?

In stave five, we see Scrooge fully engaging with the world beyond his parameters. Finally, he no longer only lives on the boundaries of life, because he is ready to have relationships with those around him. As Scrooge walks the streets in stave five, he interacts with people and smiles at them, showing a desire to no longer 'edge' the streets of London, but it is in his arrival at Fred's door that Dickens truly uses setting to highlight Scrooge's redemption. When Scrooge asks Fred 'will you let me in?', he is not only asking if he can physically be let into Fred's house, but also whether he can be let into Fred's life. After years of being harsh to his nephew, who still toasts to Scrooge despite his misanthropic ways, Scrooge's use of a question highlights an unsure tone to Scrooge's request. Dickens' hyperbole in Fred's reaction is telling the reader that integrating with those around you – family, colleagues, wider society – will always be positively received. It isn't too late for Scrooge to try with Fred, to stop existing on the edge of every setting and relationships he has in his life. This message is encapsulated in the simple phrase 'He was at home in five minutes'. In other words, Dickens is reassuring his reader that it does not take long to make amends, to come in to the warmth of 'home' if you spend your time in the 'cold and darkness' outside. So, Scrooge's physical entry into Fred's home, the first time he actually joins people beyond the 'narrow limits' of his home and his counting house, is a joyous moment for Fred, Scrooge and the reader. Dickens wants us to realise that existing on the periphery of settings and, therefore, life is a 'lonely', 'dark' and 'cold' existence, and that we can be at 'home' immediately, if we only ask and try to enter the word around us.

No evidence is used here – do you think it is needed? Does it work without specific quotations?

The candidate expertly moves between how the text is intended to be received and the text itself in this section. It shows an acute understanding of the text as a construct, always an indicator of a high level response.

Critical response

This is a sophisticated and mature exploration of what is a fundamentally difficult question. Although the candidate only really uses short quotations, their knowledge of the text and its settings ensures that the answer only ever feels exploratory, rather than offering simple or explained ideas. There is an academic style used that allows analysis to feel part of the interpretation. It is a well-structured response that always returns to the task and the overall thread of the argument.

An Inspector Calls

Ideas about gender

3.1 How does Priestley present ideas about gender in *An Inspector Calls*?

3.1.1 Clear response

Women treated as objects/commodities in line with a capitalist society. Priestley highlighting how not enough has changed 1912–1945 in terms of gender. (mainly Birling men – Eric/Mr B)	
1 'Sign or token of their self-respect' how women's attractiveness = their value	2 'But these girls aren't cheap labour – they're *people*' Mr B – commodified as labour
3 'She was pretty and a good sport' – sport makes her a game, not an individual	4 'used her [...] as if she was an animal, a thing, not a person' – sexual gain for Eric

How much more could be said about this initial metaphor? What key words could be analysed?

The candidate links well here to the bigger ideas of the play, particularly ideas around gender.

J. B. Priestley presents us with men who treat women as objects, making the men believe that clothing is an important aspect of a woman. In particular, Mr Birling describes the women's clothing as a 'sign or token of their self-respect'. This metaphor suggests to us that women only see value in their appearance, not their interactions or ability to think. This is typical in 1912, as Priestley sets his play in pre-war Britain, and so at this point, women do not have the vote and are not expected to work. Mr Birling perceiving clothing as a 'token' indicates the misogyny of many men, and indeed women, at the time who believe that a woman's appearance is their most valuable aspect. Interestingly, this links to Eva's job at Milwards where she holds an item of clothing up to her, one that she would never be able to afford, and smiles (which Sheila misreads). Whilst Priestley writes the play in the post-war period, a time in which Britain has seen the true potential of women and their ability to work and vote, the play is still set in a time where women lack a range of rights and are seen as objects. This is shown through the emphasis on their clothing, also spoken by a man, so the women's perspective is silenced. Priestley is perhaps exposing how much has changed within the 30 years between when the play is set and when it is written and encouraging the audience to accept and continue these changes.

The response is aware of the historical context both of when the play is written and when the play is set.

Furthermore, when women do work, they are not thanked or respected for their work. Sheila tells Inspector Goole, 'but these girls aren't cheap labour – they're *people*', when the Inspector tells her that there are a lot of women living in Eva's existence. Priestley is highlighting to the audience that, whilst women were working in 1912, no one valued them for their work, instead they were treated as 'cheap labour' rather than actual humans with emotion. It almost seems like Mr Birling does not want the women to have human characteristics. When he

How could these ideas all be linked together with a clearer thread to the whole response?

This second quotation is an appropriate choice to back up the candidate's original idea.

admits to dismissing Eva, he states that she had 'far too much' to say, suggesting that a woman who has an opinion about her work is a problem. Notably, Eva is not bad at her job as, at the time of the strike, Birling is considering promoting her. Her work rate is irrelevant if she wants to have a say, and so Mr Birling is willing to dismiss her because she goes beyond the boundaries of 'cheap labour'. He doesn't want to have to see her as a person because then he might have to review how much he pays her. Priestley is showing how being a woman means that different expectations are placed on you and that you are expected to remain quiet and not ask questions.

Many of the men in the play treat women as a game or something they have to figure out and discover. Arthur makes comments to the family regarding the various things they will soon learn about women, suggesting women are cryptic and unusual, but also that men can gain an understanding of all of them someday. This is further exemplified when Eric says that Eva was 'pretty and a good sport'. The metaphor of a woman as a 'sport' not only suggests that Eric views her as a game but also indicates a more general view of women at the time. It might imply that Eric considers Eva as a competition, something that he could eventually win, with the prize most likely being related to sex with her. This again gives us the idea that women were treated as objects, or that they had little importance in society for anything beyond how attractive they might be. Interestingly, Eric begins with the adjective 'pretty' as his focus is on her appearance rather than her intellect or personality – this links to how many of the men talk about women in the play, and even to how Sheila sees herself. Priestley is questioning the expectations of gender in the Edwardian era and illuminating any changes that have occurred during the post-war years.

Finally, we see that women have their humanity taken from them in the eyes of many of the men in the play. This is particularly clear in the way Eric treats Eva. Often people sympathise with Eric as he changes by the end of the play, but we might argue that his treatment of Eva is worse than the other men in the play. As the Inspector leaves, he tells Eric that in his relationship with Eva he 'used her [...] as if she were an animal, a thing, not a person.' Priestley highlights how women are not treated as humans, but instead can be considered as an object or 'thing'. The list of three exaggerates how Eric's treatment did not allow Eva to be treated equally or even as a human, but instead, he treated her in an inhumane way. The verb 'used' develops the idea that she is an object, something that he can use and then discard once she has fulfilled his needs. Priestley wants to show that women are more than objects or animals; they are humans and should be treated in that way.

> This third paragraph offers a clear idea and it is backed up with a well-selected piece of evidence.

> **How could these comments about society be made more specific, with more appropriate vocabulary?**

> The candidate explains more than one interpretation of a character here, which fleshes out a clear initial response.

> **Could there be better layers of analysis explored here?**

3.1.2 Thoughtful response

Overall, in *An Inspector Calls*, the women are presented as objects. The men throughout the play, especially Mr Birling, do not fully treat the women as humans with emotions and their own characters. Priestley criticises the men in the audience and society at the time for this sexist treatment of women.

Before Inspector Goole's arrival, Mr Birling offers a clearly sexist view of women, shared with the younger male members of his family. He says that what women wear is a 'sign or token of their self-respect.' This is commented on because he has left Sheila and Mrs Birling discussing clothing, while the men then discuss business in another room. This staging by Priestley is a clear sign of the lack of importance of the two women within the family home (despite Mrs Birling technically being Mr Birling's social superior). The metaphor of a 'token' highlights how women have to use their appearance to gain respect and attention from those around them, particularly men, and that any of this is just a 'token' in reaction to how they look. This emphasis on clothing clearly foreshadows what we learn happened at Milwards between Sheila and Eva; throughout the play, clothing is closely associated with respect and value. Evidently, it becomes a 'token' for Eva that she cannot afford, as a result of losing her job to Mr Birling. Indeed, the way Eva is treated is not just an example of one individual in Edwardian society, as Priestley is drawing the audience's attention to the treatment of women of all classes – they are all 'potty' about clothing which might earn them 'self-respect', believes Mr Birling – or, they are all patronised by men who see themselves as superior to all women just because of their gender.

Women are further presented as objects when Mr Birling explains his reasons for having Eva Smith fired. He does not hold himself responsible at all, believing no blame rests on him, claiming he was 'quite justified'. Despite this, it appears that not only the Inspector disagrees with him: Sheila states that 'these girls aren't cheap labour – they're *people*.' The emphasis on 'people' draws the audience's attention to how Mr Birling dehumanises the women who work for him, believing they are objects and only 'labour'. Furthermore, the pause would ensure that the actor would hold the audience before exclaiming 'they're *people*' in an almost frustrated tone, one which grows with Sheila throughout the play. This ideology does not align with the capitalist views that Sheila has been raised with and the views, most likely, of the majority of the audience. By simplifying it into 'labour' versus 'people', Priestley is making clear that human beings cannot be treated as simply a workforce. Throughout the whole play, this is highlighted by Eva Smith's character, who is used as a vehicle to illustrate to the post-war audience the reality of the lives of these working class women. She becomes a symbol of the mistreatment of these women, and Sheila offering a more socialist viewpoint is interesting, as it shows her views changing and moving away from her parents, perhaps encouraging the audience that their views could also change.

Treating women as more than objects, as complex beings with lives that are intertwined with the upper class, allows Priestley to encourage empathy for these women, stopping the audience from seeing them as a group of 'labour' and instead as individual 'people'.

Women continue to be seen as objects and not individuals when Eric explains his interactions with Eva Smith and his perception of her. When he states that 'she was pretty and a good sport' he highlights the sexism of many men in the Edwardian era. It is clear that his treatment of Eva as a game or something to win is not something that is exclusive to Eric, but more likely symbolic of much of the upper class – or, indeed, any class – men of the era. The belief that women are something to win is clear in the metaphor of Eva as 'sport', implying she played along with his advances, but also that she was a game that he wanted to play. The adjective 'pretty' also links back to the clothing mentioned previously, as it is the aesthetic aspects of Eric that Eva finds pleasing, rather than anything about her personality or behaviour. Whilst this explanation of Eva is given when Eric is being questioned about their continued relationship, it is also evidence of the way he treated her on their first night together, where he turned 'nasty' and 'threatened to make a row'. This behaviour is complicated but we might consider Eric's choices are a reaction to Eva's attempt to reject Eric's advances. His long-established sexism, something he has been taught as he has grown up, tells him that he is superior to Eva, and he can therefore force himself on her if he wants to. Priestley criticises this male behaviour and highlights the longer-term dangers of sexism – it makes men believe they are entitled to every part of a woman, and that they are a 'sport' to win.

Finally, women being treated as objects is clear in the Inspector's final speech, and the sexism faced by many women of the time is evident in his final words. He tells Eric that she 'used' Eva, 'as if she was an animal, a thing, not a person'. This indicates how men like Eric – his is symbolic of those in the upper class like him – see a woman's gender as an advantage to 'use' them, and that they almost don't count as human. This list of three exemplifies how men constantly mistreat women, and take away their humanity. Eric does this when he assaults her, but then continues to treat her as an object as he visits her for sexual gratification rather than for building a relationship. This objectification of women is evident for all of the men in the play, and it is a clear message which Priestley is reinforcing

> There is careful examination of how the metaphor is used here, with a range of detailed comments.

> **How does the candidate integrate evidence to prove their ideas in this paragraph?**

> The quotations throughout are used to support the interpretations given. This one is particularly successful.

At this point the candidate uses the term 'objectification' – how might this word have improved some of the ideas explained previously in this essay?

to the audience. The more men mistreat women and treat them as 'thing[s]', the worse humanity will become as a result. In Eva, as an example of the lower class women of Edwardian England, her mistreatment results in a tragedy. For Sheila Birling, seeing the way the men around her treat women, only pushes her away from them, and to seek change as a result. Throughout the play, it is clear that the sexism from men causes the mistreatment and objectification of women, and it is this that Priestley criticises and encourages the audience to question.

Thoughtful response
The ideas in this response join up to prove an overall argument that women are treated as objects. One key successful aspect of this response is the development of analysis to considering the whole text, whether that be the use of motifs or characters as devices, allowing the candidate to show a wider understanding. There are also detailed links made between the concepts (such as gender and class) and the historical context.

3.1.3 Critical response

This is a strong and confident opening where the candidate ensures they narrow the focus of their argument but still considers the question at length.

Inextricably both misogynistic and arrogant, the men of Priestley's *An Inspector Calls* are fuelled by a desire to exert their dominance over women. They do this by treating the women of the play as not merely objects but commodities. This commodification of an entire gender allows the men to treat them in ways which the audience may struggle to understand. In hyperbolising man's treatment of women, Priestley highlights the way women – of every class and age – suffer at the hands of men (both in 1912 and, still, in 1945).

How does this opening point clearly link to the ideas set out in the introduction?

There is exploratory comments on the effects of language choices here, rather than a focus on the terminology used.

The commodification of women begins when it becomes clear that their inherent value is enhanced by their physical appearance. When Mr Birling explains to the men that clothing is a 'sign or token' of a woman's 'self-respect', Priestley is offering the view of not one individual but many in the Edwardian era. The metaphorical 'token' almost sounds monetary too, like a woman's value can be increased by the purchase of clothing, in the same way that a doll can be enhanced by the clothing purchased for it. Priestley's irony in 'self-respect' demonstrates how Birling views women as needing to acquire respect for themselves through their clothing, as, like objects, they initially do not possess respect for themselves. Furthermore, by it being 'self-respect' Mr Birling is suggesting that women cannot ever gain respect from those around them, or that men will not respect women no matter how respectable their clothing looks. Perhaps this is not necessarily a desire to dominate women, but an almost disdain for their desire to be valued and treated with respect, something it seems Mr Birling is both unwilling and unable to give. Rooted in misogyny and hierarchy, Priestley reinforces to the audience the ways women were treated by men (both in 1912 and 1945) to only dismantle this treatment as the play goes on, offering a social critique of the contemporaneous views on gender.

How does this ending link the contextual consideration to the focus of the question?

Mr Birling finds it easy to commodify the women who work for him, as they are simply individuals who represent commerce, rather than actual humans with emotions. This becomes clearer as he attempts to justify his treatment of the women who went on strike and is crystallised in Sheila's comment: 'But these girls aren't cheap labour – they're *people*.' Significantly, Sheila's view on the women's role in Birling's factory starkly juxtaposes the views of not only her father but also her future husband, who agrees with Mr Birling's decision to not offer them a better living wage. The financial noun 'labour' juxtaposes with the more humanitarian 'people' – this juxtaposition is symbolic of the viewpoints of Sheila and Mr Birling by the end of the play, ideologies which were once aligned now growing further apart along the political spectrum. Indeed, the adjective 'cheap' returns us to the idea of women as a commodity – a product which Mr Birling feels he can buy, or pay, at the lowest possible price – rather than actual humans with a life to lead. Indeed, when he discusses the women's return ('at the old rates') it all comes down to financial leverage – getting them to work for the cheapest amount. Mr Birling's dismissal of paying the women any more money is undoubtedly fuelled by his classism, but it is also a result of his misogyny. He does not want to pay the women more because he does not believe they are *worth* any more – they are simple objects that he buys, much like the produce his factory will need. Priestley criticises many aspects of society here: the upper class, sexist men and capitalist greed that causes unfair workers' conditions. He aims these criticisms at his audience, who are likely to fall into one of these categories or at least enable this behaviour.

Treating women as a commodity is not an attitude exclusive to Mr Birling, his son, Eric has also learned from his treatment and we see this in the way he talks about Eva. Many consider his discussion of Eva to be one that shows some humanity, perhaps evident in the clear regret and guilt he feels, compounded by the realisation that his child has also been lost. The reality is though that Eric sexually assaults Eva and, even once he knows about her treatment, he states that she was 'pretty and a good sport'. Notably, this phrasing is indicative of his misogyny – something he has been raised to believe, rather than something he has been taught to question. Eric calling Eva a 'sport' commodifies her in that she becomes a game to him, which feels even more sinister when we know what he eventually did to her. A 'sport' for those in positions of power is another way to exert dominance over others, to feel competitive and elite. This desire to dominate is no doubt part of the reason Eric does what he does – he is not willing to be told 'no' by an object he considers a game to win, rather than a human who can make decisions and reject his advances. The adjective 'pretty' is interesting when we consider Mr Birling's earlier comments about 'self-respect'. Throughout the play, the motif of clothing is used to signify value and we know that Eva longs to have access to the wealthy clothing the Birlings wear (this is evident when she holds up the dress that Sheila is about to try on and smiles). However, Eva's

There is close and detailed exploration of language here. The layers of analysis support the candidate in exploring how Priestley creates various meanings, with precise terminology used to examine language.

How and why is this a successful end to this paragraph?

This opening idea shows an excellent understanding. The response has clearly grown in confidence and is now offering perceptive and personal ideas about the text.

At this point the candidate is weaving analytical comments alongside contextual appreciation in order to create exploratory and critical paragraphs.

Why is this final short reference successful in this closing line?

natural beauty is part of her tragedy. This beauty leads men in power to treat her as a 'sport' to conquer and only makes her a commodity in their eyes. Priestley forces his audience to see the inhumanity in these actions; Eric may feel remorse for his actions, but, as the Inspector states, it is 'too late' for Eva Smith.

Whilst many of the women in the play are treated as insignificant objects, it is Eva Smith who faces the worst treatment, most likely due to her class. This treatment is abundantly clear in the Inspector's final speech, where he summarises the 'chain of events' that caused her death. Each member of the family is, of course, held responsible but the comment made to Eric is significant in terms of how women have been presented as commodities, or objects, throughout the play: he 'used her [...] as if she was an animal, a thing, not a person'. The dehumanisation of Eva, and indeed all women in the play, is epitomised in these words from the Inspector. The tricolon builds from something alive in 'animal', to an object or 'thing', to something completely devoid of humanity. Priestley's use of asyndetic listing exaggerates the mistreatment of Eva here, as the audience, and indeed the gathered family, are hit with their objectification of Eva as the list continues. The verb 'used' links back to how each man treats her, and indeed women like her, as a commodity; she can be 'used' for whatever they need – sexual gratification, 'cheap labour' or 'sport' – and disposed of equally as easily. Priestley engineers this moment within the Inspector's closing speech to offer a final and clear socio-political message. As women continue to be objectified by men, and indeed society as a whole, they will begin to lose their humanity. It is humanity that we need to continue society and this dangerous message will offer the audience absolute clarity on the gender dynamics not only in Edwardian Britain but also in post-war Britain. Society needs women to prosper in all of their human complexity. If men continue to commodify women, then it is not only women but also humanity in its entirety that will suffer.

Throughout this response the candidate has used precise references which have formed an integral part of the response. They not only show thorough understanding, but allow the candidate to fully explore the text.

Here, the candidate offers convincing and mature ideas about the text's position and weight within its historical context. These ideas are held critically and with confidence.

Critical response
This is a mature and sensitive response which is able to closely consider the text's main conceptual ideas and their place within the context. The analysis – although often focused on language – considers the various effects of choices in close detail. The thread of the commodification of women is coherent throughout and offers a clear argument which is both personal and perceptive.

The Inspector as a force for good

3.2 How far does Priestley present the character of the Inspector as a force for good within the play?

mouthpiece for socialist ideologies, profound impact on post-war audience of 1945
Entrance; compare to Birling – lighting 'pink and intimate' – 'brighter and harder' – 'like bees in a hive – community and all that nonsense'; 'mind his own and look after himself and his own – and –' vs. 'give us some more light' and 'I'm on duty'; 'impression of massiveness, solidity and purposefulness [....] looking hard at the person', 'sharply'
Relationship with Eva Smith: who is he and why is he here? Draws our attention back to Eva – the Birlings see her as a 'very pretty girl' but 'several hours of agony' 'burnt her insides out, of course', insists they see Eva and all she represents – homonym
Impact on the younger generation and the hope for the future; 'not cheap labour – they're people'
What will happen if we do not change? 'we are members of one body'

3.2.1 Clear response

Within *An Inspector Calls*, the character of the Inspector holds many socialist views and enters into the world of the Birlings in order to attempt to change their rigid and often outdated opinions. The Inspector appears to be used as a device to express the views that Priestley held regarding the divide within post-war society. Priestley hoped that his audiences would recognise that, following two world wars, returning to a world where men and the wealthy ruled society would be a step in the wrong direction. Through putting these ideas into a play, it was hoped that audience members would be shocked by the behaviour of the Birlings and change their own ways if they recognised themselves within their characters.

> How does the candidate immediately ensure that they engage with the writer's intentions?

The Inspector enters the Birlings' dining room at a crucial point in the play. Mr Birling has just been explaining his own views and explains that he thinks 'a man has to mind his own business and look after himself' because he thinks it's foolish to think that people are 'all mixed up together like bees in a hive'. This simile shows Mr Birling's lack of care towards other people, specifically the poor, as what he doesn't realise is that 'bees in a hive' only work successfully because they work together and they all have an important part to play. Almost immediately, the doorbell rings in a 'sharp' tone and Birling 'stops to listen'. Mr Birling then orders Edna, his maid, to 'give us some more light'. In asking for 'more light', Birling is foreshadowing that he and his family will become more exposed as they will be able to be seen far better, yet at this point in the play, Mr Birling does not think that he has anything that he can actually be exposed for. When the Inspector enters, the stage directions at the start of act 1 state that the 'lighting should be pink and intimate' until Inspector Goole arrives and then it becomes 'brighter and harder'.

> The candidate's focus on specific language devices used here is clear and well explained.

> Can you identify where the candidate has used stage directions to support their ideas?

This change from being soft and comfortable to harsh and 'harder' could also suggest that things are about to get tougher for the Birling family and society, as a whole, if they do not listen to and learn from the Inspector.

The candidate has good knowledge of the play and can link ideas across from across the acts.

Explaining that he is 'on duty', the Inspector is responsible for investigating the death of Eva Smith the 'young woman who died in the Infirmary'. Whilst he tells the Birlings that he is a police officer, much later in the play, the family try to suggest he is a 'hoax' and not a 'real Police Inspector'. The Birling family become slightly obsessive over whether the Inspector is real, yet this shows their inability to realise that they have done something wrong. Even describing his visit as a 'hoax' shows that the Birling family are subconsciously using crime lexicon, showing that deep down they know that they have exhibited criminal behaviour even though it might not have been related to this specific death, but they are unable to accept or understand what they have done. Importantly, the Inspector explains to the family in pointed language that 'she'd swallowed a lot of strong disinfectant. Burnt her inside out, of course' and his utterance 'of course' suggests that he is used to hearing of, or seeing, girls (and generally) people in terrible conditions in a way that the Birling family has not.

The candidate uses terminology to explain the writer's choices clearly and accurately. There is a clear attempt to explain the writer's intentions.

What is the effect of using the adverb 'ostensibly' here? What does it show about the candidate's knowledge?

Whilst ostensibly the Inspector is trying to investigate the death of Eva Smith, more importantly he is trying to show the Birlings and other middle-upper class people that they need to change. Priestley wanted society to adopt more socialist views where they looked after one another much more widely. This is why the Inspector's impact on the two younger Birlings can show that he is a force for good within the play. Even within act 1, Eric explains that Mr Birling 'could have kept her on instead of throwing her out' and the violent verb 'throwing' shows just how much force Mr Birling used when removing Eva from his workplace because 'she'd had a lot to say'. The way that Priestley shows the differences between Sheila and Eric and Mr and Mrs Birling continues into the play as Sheila recognises that 'these girls aren't cheap labour – they're people' as she uses much more socialist language where she refers to girls like Eva as 'people' but her father considers them 'labour' as he cannot move away from the language of the workplace. Specifically, the idea that the girls are 'labour' is important here; they work for him and provide for him and he does not have to do anything back for them. Importantly, at the end of the play, Eric and Sheila are firmly of the same view as the Inspector as Sheila explains 'we drove that girl to commit suicide'. Sheila uses the first person plural pronoun as she recognises that they are all part of the 'mess'.

How could the candidate ensure that their writing is more analytical here to support them in moving to the next level?

The candidate links back to the focus of the question here to ensure that their writing is on track to response to the set task.

Priestley uses the Inspector as a force for good in the play. Before he leaves the stage, he warns the Birling family that 'we are responsible for each other' and it is the key idea of being responsible that Priestley wanted to highlight. By Sheila and Eric taking responsibility for their own actions, it offers an audience and Priestley hope that a brighter, more socialist future could come to pass.

> **Clear response**
> This response is clear as the candidate explains reasons as to why the Inspector can be seen for a force for good. The candidate makes continual reference to the text throughout their response and uses terminology accurately when quoting from the play. At times, the writing feels a little narrative as the candidate describes what happens, yet this is an approach that has been taken to ensure that there is sufficient coverage of the text when responding to the set task. The candidate refers back to the task within their response and attempts to refer to the writer's intentions at several, appropriate points.

3.2.2 Thoughtful response

Often viewed as a mouthpiece for Priestley, the titular character of *An Inspector Calls* exhibits strong socialist views and possesses a desire for change throughout his time on stage within the play. Following two world wars, society in 1945 had experienced vast social upheaval and citizens had become much more reliant on the ability to work together. Through the Inspector, Priestley expresses his keen desire for society to not revert to the heady capitalism of a by-gone era where men, and those in elevated positions in society, continued to pass rules and govern in a way that excluded the many and provided for the few. As a character device, the Inspector is designed to be a force for good within the play as he encourages the characters to reflect on their own socially, morally and legally questionable behaviour, which also allows for the audience to look within themselves to question whether they too need to re-evaluate their actions towards others.

> This opening shows that the candidate has an awareness of the play's context whilst using this to support their understanding of the demands of the set essay.

> **How does the candidate draw our awareness to the importance of the text type?**

The Inspector's purpose within the play is clear: he is there to draw our attention back to Eva Smith the 'young girl' who 'died in the infirmary'. Without the voice of the Inspector, Eva could easily be forgotten by the Birling family who, on a larger scale, represent those middle-upper class families who believed that they only had 'to mind [their] own business and look after [themselves]'. The stage directions in the opening of act 1 reflect this desire to draw the attention of the Birlings and the audience to Eva. We are told that the lighting should be 'pink and intimate', up until the arrival of the Inspector when it switches to be 'brighter and harder'. The contrast in this lighting design itself is interesting when considering the Inspector's role. The presence of the Inspector alone is what transforms the family's cosy setting into one much more representative of a police investigation room or even a morgue. We should note that this change in lighting only shifts at the Inspector's arrival too, not just when he begins speaking, which further serves to reinforce the idea that it is his 'impression of massiveness' that causes a change and not what he says. This further serves to show that the Inspector is encouraging the Birlings and the audience to see Eva, to see what they have done as opposed to just listening to him, which is potentially why the amount of speech that the Inspector actually has is incredibly limited up until his parting diatribe.

> This confident style of writing shows the candidate's awareness and understanding of the play and its purpose.

> **How does the candidate use textual references within this paragraph to show their secure understanding of the play?**

> There is extended discussion of one idea here that helps to develop the content of the writing.

How does the candidate link the opening of this paragraph to the close of the previous to ensure cohesion?

When the Inspector does speak, it is concisely and directly. Explaining that 'she swallowed a lot of strong disinfectant. Burnt her inside out, of course', the Inspector does not shy away from the bleak outcome of Eva's life. There is potential here to suggest that this is because, whilst hearing these words may spark a sense of horror in an audience, and indeed the Birling family, this is nothing in comparison to how Eva had been treated throughout her life. It could be suggested that the Inspector feels that it is his 'duty' to highlight the suffering of so many young, working class women who suffered the same treatment. The adverbial utterance 'of course' appears to suggest that this type of suffering is nothing new to the Inspector; a social ghoul whose omniscient presence is largely suggested by his homonym Goole: G – double O – L – E. This serves to set him further outside of the social conventions of the middle class Birling family. To consider the Inspector as a force for good also demands that Priestley's secondary homonym of 'Eva Smith' be considered. It can be no accident that Priestley names his voiceless victim after the first female in the Bible, suggesting that she is representative of many 'millions and millions' of other Eva Smiths. It is this that makes the character device of the Inspector a force for good as he actively tries to educate both the audience and the Birlings on the plight of these women living among them.

The candidate chooses to focus on a singular technique used multiple times here in order to deepen analysis and contribute to their overall response to the task.

The Inspector's success in his attempt to educate the Birlings is much more profitable when he deals with the younger generation who, by his own account, are more 'impressionable'. Even as early as the end of act 1, Sheila is able to recognise that she will 'never, never do [what she did] again to anybody' which is in sharp contrast even to her own fiancé, who asserts a similar position to Mr Birling as he claims 'I don't come into this suicide business. The noun 'business' here is not only used as a euphemism for the girl's suicide but also shows Gerald's inability to break away from the 'hard headed' economic lexicon that mirrors his father in law's. Priestley's juxtaposing language to show the differences between the younger and older generations within the play again capitalises on the motif of finance as Sheila proclaims that 'these girls aren't cheap labour – they're people' whereby she distinctly highlights the difference in her own attitude to girls like Eva in stark contrast to the older members of her family.

Making links between different points within the play, and comparisons between different characters, helps to demonstrate a precise understanding of the main ideas within the text.

References are continually well selected for impact.

How does the candidate make structural references here to end their essay in a cohesive manner?

Ostensibly, at the end of the play, 'nothing really happened' to the behaviour of the Birlings, yet the cyclical structure of the play goes some way to suggest that this doomed cycle of poorly treating others in society needs to stop else the same consequences will continue to play out. The final moments of the play see the 'telephone ring[ing] sharply' as a pointed reminder that this painful questioning of the Birlings will indeed continue until they all adopt a similar approach to Sheila and Eric. As a force for good, the Inspector plays a vital role in ensuring that both the Birlings, and the audience beyond the fourth wall, truly understand the serious weight of their blinkered, capitalist actions.

> **Thoughtful response**
> This response deals with ideas in a confident manner through a secure written tone and voice that is maintained throughout. The candidate has an increasingly thoughtful appreciation of how meanings and ideas are conveyed through language structure and form. Relevant subject terminology is used accurately and appropriately to develop ideas and engagement with the text through the use of precise references is secure throughout. Whilst the candidate does make reference to the contextual backdrop of the play, it would be beneficial to see this woven into the response more rather than being a singular point of reference at the opening of the candidate's essay.

3.2.3 Critical response

Whether you view him as a detective in a Cluedo-esque drama, a police officer doing his 'duty' or a 'socialist or some sort of crank', the 'impression of massiveness' that Inspector Goole leaves on an audience, and indeed some members of the Birling family, is undeniable within the play. Often viewed as a character who is the mouthpiece of J.B. Priestley himself, his words and aims hold a socialist direction as he chides those who fail to acknowledge and respond to their social responsibility. Set in 1912, yet written in 1945, this retrospective knowledge of the world held by Priestley ripples through the drama, reminding audiences of how singular and self-serving society was before two world wars that helped to blur the edges of the once clear-cut social classes, later giving rise to the Labour Party who aimed to support the needs of the many through their parliamentary reign. The Inspector within the play is undoubtedly a force for good. He acts as a spokesman for the voiceless Eva Smith and can be seen expressing Eva's unconscious fury at those who have rendered her a victim. The Inspector, through the will of Priestley, desires to remind people of their civic duty and restore a sense of 'community' to the Birlings' microcosm of middle class England.

> This personal and bold opening responds almost immediately to the set task whilst confidently exploring how this is achieved.

> How does the candidate ensure that the reader understands that the Inspector is a device acting as an extension of Priestley's views?

As the Birlings are characters trapped within the four walls of the dramatic space, the naturalistic set and lighting that Priestley indicates should be used have multiple purposes. Firstly, the lighting undergoes a transition from 'pink and intimate' to 'brighter and harder' when the Inspector first enters their world on stage. This serves two purposes: not only could this initial lighting design suggest that the 'pink' hue represents the Birlings' view of the world as rose-tinted, yet the fact that it changes so very quickly could allow an audience to see that their views also need to shift at a rapid pace. The 'brighter and harder' lighting feels reminiscent of a police examination room or even a morgue, suggesting that the Birlings will be examined and scrutinised with no shadows to further lurk in. Secondly, the fact that the set is so naturalistic could also suggest the limitations of the Birlings' world and subsequent mindset – they are stuck. Not only can the Birlings (as the embodiment of the upper and ruling classes of the time) resist their own social confines, but they are also unable to escape their 'responsibility' for what they did to Eva and, most likely, 'millions' of other young women in her position.

> How does the candidate use clear discourse markers to develop their ideas?

> The candidate makes a perceptive point here that links the content to the context and does so through careful understanding of not just the text, but the format too.

If the Inspector is to represent a force for good, then his juxtaposed counterpart, Mr Birling, can surely be viewed as an outdated force that Priestley and the H. G. Wells' and Bernard Shaws of the world also wished to eradicate. Their juxtaposed views are aptly conveyed through their speech and an audience is expected to note the painful undertones of Mr Birling's assertions. Before the Inspector's entrance, Mr Birling suggests that the idea of being 'mixed up together like bees in a hive' is utter 'nonsense' that does not appeal to him. Unfortunately, this is just the start of Birling's foolish characterisation by Priestley as his use of the simile here supports the idea that Birling really is blinkered to how the world outside of his home truly operates. He fails to acknowledge that the 'community' of bees means by their very nature means that they are all 'mixed up' and that all bees play a particular role. Without the worker bees, the queen bee (who Birling would surely liken himself to) fails to thrive. For her to flourish, the other bees need to understand their roles and be allowed to perform them. This highlights the forgotten strata in society that Birling is unable to, or does not want to, see. He foolishly fails to acknowledge that without individuals working together, the system of 'labour' would collapse entirely. This anti-civic language is contrasted by the Inspector who performs his 'duty' and, later in the play, commands Birling to not 'stammer and yammer at me, man'. Not only does the Inspector's use of apocryphal language here appear to mock Birling's provincial accent, reminding him of his roots, but also mimics the sound emanating from Birling. It is as though the Inspector suggests that Mr Birling just expresses noise and not sensible musings. We must also note the fact that the Inspector also only refers to him as 'man' as he subtly depersonalises Birling before Priestley's stage directions later tell us that Birling speaks 'savagely' as he is transformed from a 'hard-headed practical man of business' to a wild and feral animal-like 'man'.

Making the other characters actually see Eva Smith and her pitiful demise, the Inspector's use of language again is used to strike a chord with the characters. The Inspector describes how she 'swallowed a lot of strong disinfectant. Burnt her insides out, of course' where his graphic imagery of burnt insides quite literally commands the family to imagine her with nothing within her, rendering her some sort of shell. This is how the Birlings, in reality, treated her and many others. Eva Smith is no more than cheap labour to Mr Birling, which is something that Priestley's homonym further reinforces. The Biblical allusion to God's female creation could highlight that Eva is not a person to the Birlings, just a version of a character from a book – they treat her with the same level of detachment. Interestingly, Eva is shown to swallow disinfectant, a chemical product used to cleanse surfaces of dirt and germs. Is Priestley, yet again, making a political standpoint that the kind of social cleansing that the ruling classes attempted to perform for their own gain was outdated, inhumane and needed to stop?

The force of the Inspector is felt most keenly by Sheila and Eric within the play. It is Sheila who first comments that it is a 'rotten shame' that Eva died, potentially hinting at the decaying insides of the middle to upper classes. Sheila also responds to the Inspector's taunting by claiming that 'these girls aren't cheap labour – they're people'; an audience can hear the difference in the language choices made by Sheila and the Inspector as opposed to the older generation. Sheila's assertion that they are 'girls' and not women could suggest that they are young and can become the future, whereas her father has always seen them as 'labour', as someone to task with the un-thanked, joyless work that elevates him to an even higher social standing. The Inspector comments that the younger generation of Birlings and society, in general, are more impressionable, offering an audience hope that the generation coming through could help to change the landscape of Britain for the better going forward.

As the Inspector departs, his political diatribe reminds us of the prophetic warnings of the Old Testament that a time will come when punishment will be heaved across the land if 'men will not learn [their] lesson'. As a force for good, the Inspector sets out to give the Birlings the opportunity to rectify the errors of their way and become 'members of one body' with the collective noun 'members' suggesting that the Birlings must subscribe to this way of thinking and not just be the passengers of change. The change in Sheila and Eric illustrates that it is possible to step out of the existence into which one was born and that without doing this the bell will continue to 'sharply' ring again for them. This ringing of both the doorbell and telephone can be seen to echo the funeral bell in John Donne's 'Meditation XVII' as the 'bell tolls for thee' who fail to perform their civic duty and begin to savour the challenge of supporting others. The Inspector hopes to deliver society, through the Birlings, from this demise as he seeks to offer a good and better future for all.

> **How does the candidate link the text to the context here?**

> The candidate's fluent expression and links to external ideas demonstrate their confident engagements with the meanings and messages of the play.

> **How is cohesion ensured right to the very end?**

Critical response

This response is not only confident, but perceptive as it tackles challenging ideas about society with maturity and sensitivity. The candidate successfully makes multiple suggestions about the possibilities of the text's meanings and does so through a suggestive tone. The response is a cohesive evaluation of all of the evidence presented to the candidate by the play which is expertly supported by their knowledge of supporting texts and a sensitive understanding of the context. The candidate is clearly well-read and brings their knowledge to their response. The writer's methods accompanied by subject terminology are explored at the highest level. The candidate clearly introduces their own style of writing and we get a real sense of fluency through the vocabulary and grammatical choices that are made to express their views.

Mr Birling as an example of all men in society

3.3 To what extent do you think Priestley uses Mr Birling as an example of all men in society at the time?

3.3.1 Critical response

Mr Birling is an example of the older generation of men at the time but, perhaps, also of all of humanity's flaws: greed, gluttony, wrath, pride. These blind him. Priestley is warning about morality vs immorality, rather than any specific gender flaws.	
Greed – Mr Birling's treatment of the workers is due to his capitalist greed.	'mixed up together like bees in a hive' views community as 'nonsense' because he is greedy and reluctant to share wealth. 'Lower costs and higher prices' – his greed leads to others lacking.
Pride – Mr Birling's hubris blinds him to reality. Almost satirical in his ideals.	'unsinkable, absolutely unsinkable' 'don't want war' – dramatic irony, pride blinds him – in his speeches Priestley ridicules him (and those like him).
Wrath – Birling is angered by the Inspector so much that this prevents him seeing the truth.	'wretched girl's suicide' 'if you don't come down hard on these people they'd soon be asking for the earth' – innate anger/frustration at Inspector and poor.
End – moral shift? Or still motivated by pride/greed.	'I'd give thousands – yes, thousands' offers the wrong thing, more worried about damaging pride in 'public scandal' than any genuine remorse. Entirely corrupt.

How is does the candidate place the emphasis on the big ideas of the play right at the start?

Flawed, blinded and ultimately unchangeable, Mr Birling's character is ostensibly complex. The reality is that he is characterised by the flaws that seep into all of humanity: the seven deadly sins. It is reductive to consider Mr Birling as simply a symbol of men or the upper class. Instead, he represents the immorality of humanity and, unfortunately, unlike the historical morality play format, Mr Birling is unable to change and redeem himself. In this presentation, Priestley warns his post-war audience of the dangers of constant immoral behaviour and the impact these actions can have beyond one's immediate sphere of influence.

Immediately this response uses a wide range of evidence that is integrated successfully into the ideas explored.

Deeply consumed by his own greed, Mr Birling's justification of his treatment of others is driven by his capitalist ideology. As a character who believes in a world where a man 'has to look after himself', Mr Birling's greed has an impact on many of the people around him. He may believe it is important to consider his 'family too' but the reality is that his greed affects the way the family live their lives too, and so his immorality and sin spreads beyond his own actions. Mr Birling dismisses the idea of 'community' and calls it 'nonsense' – the simile of people working together 'like bees in a hive' only illuminating his own ignorance of what might happen if people do work together. His greed is highlighted particularly before the arrival of the Inspector, where he tells the assembled listeners that he will push for 'lower costs and higher prices'. This moment starkly highlights Mr Birling's greed, but also how it will have repercussions for others; for him to make more money and gain profit from 'prices' he must keep his 'costs' low. The reality, as we discover through the plight of Eva, is that the 'costs' he cuts so ruthlessly are human lives, the cost of people living with food and a roof, pushing the women of Edwardian Britain to become 'alone, friendless, almost penniless, desperate'. The harsh juxtaposition of the comparatives 'lower' and 'higher' reveal Mr Birling's ignorance in terms of how his greed infests others. For him to make money, others must lose out and he struggles to realise this, even at the play's close. His greed is a harsh reminder to the post-war audience watching, having suffered from the greed that generated world wars and the Great Depression, that sins such as avarice can only result in damage in other areas of society. Of course, Priestley establishes a blatantly socialist message by deconstructing the greed of a hyperbolised capitalist character and highlighting the way his greed impacts others.

Mr Birling's hubris is utilised by Priestley to exaggerate and ridicule those who remain blinded to reality. Another sin committed by Birling (and, arguably, by all of the family in various ways) is that of pride. The potential damage to Birling's pride is what fuels his desire to prevent 'scandal' and believe in the 'hoax' in the closing act. Priestley creates a character who attracts ridicule, and some of Birling's proclamations in act 1 are almost satirical. Priestley spotlights his pride as he mentions the potential 'knighthood' to Gerald, a way of boosting his own ego in the presence of someone with more status than him. Priestley engineers several moments of dramatic irony to further ridicule Mr Birling, encouraging the 1945 audience to see Birling's pride as something that prevents him from seeing the inevitable reality. His certainty that the Titanic is 'unsinkable', that the world will be in a phase of 'prosperity' in 1940, and – perhaps most damaging in front of a Russian audience who were just recovering from WWII – his complete belief that 'the Germans don't want war', all serve to make Birling a laughable figure. This hubris and complete lack of awareness of current affairs and the reality of 1912 are all condemned by Priestley. Yes, an audience may be encouraged to laugh, but the question must also be turned on themselves: did society's immoral actions and pride lead to a financial crash and two world wars? Most importantly, what can be done in 1945 to prevent this again? Of course, Britain answered these questions when a general election saw a landslide Labour Party majority. Clearly, both the public and Priestley were seeking a society where pride and greed aren't in abundance.

How are contextual comments interweaved into the response here?

The level of analysis here is critical and exploratory. The effects of methods are consistently detailed.

How are short quotations integrated here to show a thorough knowledge of the play?

The response moves successfully from detailed analysis of dramatic choices, through to contextual relevance, to consider the various effects on the audience. This is an extremely confident and convincing paragraph.

The conceptual approach to this question is brought together here. The candidate ensures they offer a strong, coherent argument in response to the whole text rather than moments within it.

How does this exploration of effects add to the overall argument from the introduction?

The evidence picked here is judicious – each references is selected in order to support the overall argument created.

How does the candidate bring together the argument in these final sentences?

Birling as a representation of the sins of humanity continues when we consider his angry reactions to the Inspector throughout the play. Moments of wrath occur when Mr Birling's pride or greed is questioned, and it is through these complex intertwining of the various sins of humanity that we begin to see how Mr Birling forces us to question our own morals. Mr Birling feigns interest in Eva's path but then tries to move the Inspector away from the topic, calling Eva a 'wretched girl' – this ambitious adjective potentially meaning that he sees her as unfortunate, but more likely hinting at his disgust at her lifestyle. Notably, the adverb 'angrily' is used as a stage direction for Mr Birling 17 times, often in consecutive lines spoken by Mr Birling, establishing that his wrath is not something he is able to suppress. In fact, at times the actor playing him is directed to stare or look 'angrily' at different characters, again offering the idea that his immoral behaviour is directed at others and he is unaware of the consequences of his sinful actions. Mr Birling states that 'if you don't come down hard on these people they'd soon be asking for the earth', and this highlights his deep-rooted anger towards those in poverty. The metaphor wanting the 'earth' suggests Mr Birling's belief that the poor want everything, even his own property, rather than simple things like a small pay rise, or enough to buy food. Here Birling's anger is fuelled by his greed and pride; he believes that the poor must be treated in a 'hard' way otherwise they might take from him. This innate wrath reaches a climax in the moments where Eric and Mr Birling become physical, and Mr Birling's anger towards the poor, and then the Inspector, becomes anger towards his family, those he claimed he wanted to look out for. Priestley criticises those in positions of wealth and power who direct their anger towards others rather than the system itself, and it is clear that Priestley's political anger is steeped throughout the play, as he forces the audience to observe Mr Birling's various flaws and wish to never commit such immoral actions.

The final act makes it abundantly clear that Mr Birling never intends to learn from his sins or seek atonement for his various immoral behaviours. His only concern is whether the facts of the evening will get out, create a 'public scandal,' or damage the reputation that he has built through the demise of others. Again, we see a man dictated by his own pride and greed, and he still lacks any moral change. When the Inspector attempts to remind him of what he did, he tells the Inspector 'I'd give thousands – yes, thousands'. The repetition of the hyperbolic 'thousands' almost makes this offer seem fantastical, like Birling's moral shift takes us into the fantasy world. The stilted speech at this moment, with the dashes indicating his pauses, just serve to highlight the desperation in his speech. But he is not offering the money to seek moral retribution or to fix the way Eva is treated – his offer of money is just a desire to protect his pride, the belief that he can make the situation go away by paying money, rather than being a better human being and making more morally sound choices. Mr Birling is the epitome of all that is wrong with humanity in the period between when the play is set and when it is first performed: he is corrupt, sinful, greedy, proud and angry. But so are many members of the human race at this time, as they fought with 'fire and blood and anguish' and left behind the compassion that made them human. Priestley offers his audience a stark message: the Mr Birlings of this world lead society to chaos and destruction. The only way to prevent this carnage is to choose a more humane, moral way of living and to reject sinful actions in the country's – and indeed the world's – past.

Critical response

It would be easy to respond to this question by working through key events to do with Mr Birling however, by focusing on the flaws/sins of humanity, the candidate gives themselves a conceptual framework to consider Priestley's wider exploration of the human condition. This supports the candidate in offering a perceptive and convincing response which also closely analyses the writer's key methods and their various effects.

Responsibility

3.4 To what extent is *An Inspector Calls* a play that focus on responsibility?

3.4.1 Critical response

Social responsibility and personal responsibility. The Inspector's core purpose is to demonstrate the need for others to take responsibility for themselves, their actions and the impact that these have on others (socialism).	
1. **The Inspector**: promotes the idea of social responsibility: 'She needed not only money, but advice, sympathy, friendliness' 'alone, friendless, almost penniless, desperate' 'They wanted the rates raised [...] I refused, of course' 'my duty to keep labour costs down'	2. **The men**: all use her in some way. Patriarchal society and a sense of entitlement. 'A man has to mind his own business and look after himself and his own—' 'I want you to understand that I didn't install her there so that I could make love to her'; 'I became at once the most important person in her life' (G) 'I insisted on giving her enough money to keep her going'; 'you're not the kind of father a chap could go to when he's in trouble' (E)
3. **The women**: do not use her, but use their power to be spiteful and vindictive. They do not have the same levels of power as men. Not a 'deserving case'; 'a girl of that sort'; 'ridiculous airs'	4. **Eva** is the product of a lack of responsibility (both social and personal). She tries to take responsibility for herself and others, but this is negatively impacted upon by those who have power. 'It's what happened to the girl and what we all did to her that matters'

How does the candidate identify the main questions of the task and set out to challenge them within their opening paragraph?

With an overriding moral imperative, Priestley's *An Inspector Calls* attempts to highlight the consequences of a society and its people who fail to take responsibility for themselves, their actions, and the impact that those actions have on others. Set in 1912, Priestley's political diatribe attempts to encourage audiences to embrace the socialist views emerging in the post-war era of 1945 that saw society and its citizens adopt much more inclusive views as a result of the collective trauma that they had faced at the hands of two world wars. The theme of responsibility is arguably the backbone of the play's messages with each character acting as a device through which Priestley can explore how different attitudes and mindsets can impact others and the society of the future.

The candidate here seeks to clarify their response to the set terms in the task. They also are very clear that they understand the writer's intentions.

When considering the theme of responsibility, it is important to acknowledge the difference between social responsibility and personal responsibility. Personal responsibility can be seen to be the extent to which individuals take responsibility for their own actions, which arguably leads to social responsibility

– the way in which individuals respond to the needs of others. So often throughout this play, an audience can view the way in which characters who fail to take responsibility for their own actions lead to these aforementioned actions subsequently having pejorative impacts on others.

Priestley chooses to open his play by presenting an audience with the Birling family led by the 'hard headed, practical man of business' that is Mr Birling himself. Interestingly, Mr Birling appears to understand what the idea of responsibility is, yet his responsibilities lie solely with his and his family's interests. Before the Inspector's arrival, Birling comments that 'a man has to mind his own business and look after himself and his own–', which allows an audience to recognise that much of Arthur's priorities lie with his sense of self. The repetition of the possessive pronoun 'his' allows Priestley to demonstrate that many of Arthur's views are to do with him taking possession of what he feels is owed to him, and this also enables Priestley to highlight his self-serving capitalist mindset that he ultimately seeks to show as his ultimate character flaw. If we are to view Mr Birling as the antagonist of the socialist cause, then the character of Inspector Goole can be viewed as the heroic protagonist of the morality play. His entrance is marked by the 'sharp ring' of the doorbell that cuts directly across Birling's speech, foreshadowing the way that the Inspector will 'sharp[ly]' contradict Mr Birling's views as he attempts to persuade him and his family that their social modes of operation are outdated and, quite frankly, irresponsible. As a metaphorical duel between the social outlooks begins to unfold between Birling and Inspector Goole, Priestley clearly attempts to characterise Birling as a foolish and spiteful character through his use of dramatic irony to convey his laughable views that 'the Germans don't want war' and that the 'Titanic is unsinkable'. An audience would be well versed in the understanding that two world wars threatened the existence of Europe as we have come to know it, alongside being aware of the tragedy of the Titanic. As such, this hyperbolic use of dramatic irony is an attempt to foreground Birling's views as ones that should not be believed and valued, as an audience is encouraged to find an affinity with the Inspector's words that encourage social responsibility instead.

In the patriarchal society of 1912, it is little surprise that the victim of this story is a working class woman. It is even less of a surprise that whilst she is treated poorly by members of the classes above her, it is the male figures with whom she came into contact who used her in some way for their own personal gain. Birling asserts his position that he takes no responsibility for the girl's suicide because she, and others, 'wanted the rates raised' to which he almost seems to boast that 'I refused, of course'. What an audience can see here is that the death of a young woman has ultimately occurred due to greed and a desire for 'lower costs' and 'higher prices'; the utterance of 'of course' appears to suggest is a 'chain of events' that is to be expected. Birling's use of juxtaposition when he asserts that it is his 'duty to keep labour costs down'

This analysis is successful as the candidate links an understanding of language to the main ideas within the play.

How does this response blend language and structural analysis?

Note how many times the candidate references deliberate choices by the writer. This shows that the candidate understands that the play is a construct.

The response here starts to weave in references to the other main themes of the play such as gender and social class.

allows Priestley to further remove Birling from any real sense of responsibility that he should have. Not only does Birling imitate the Inspector's language as he chooses to use the socialist noun 'duty' to explain his business manifesto, but he pairs it with the idea that he will keep the 'labour costs down' which consequently disadvantages those who were in most need of financial support (something that the later-elected Labour Party would seek to offer those in need). This further sets Birling in opposition to Inspector Goole who comments that 'she needed not only money but also advice, sympathy, friendliness' as Goole, the embodiment of socialism, recognises that 'money' is only one thing that people had a responsibility to show others. The qualities found in the asyndetic list of 'advice, sympathy, friendliness' are acutely bound up with what it means to be human. Subsequently, suggesting that Birling, and those like him, deprive others in society of basic human needs serves to highlight that he shows not a shred of social responsibility, which is what ultimately renders him socially villainous within this play.

Believing themselves to be chivalrous in their treatment of Eva Smith, the two younger males of the play, Eric and Gerald appear to recognise their actions towards Eva yet also attempt to justify them in order to atone for their treatment of the 'girl'. Gerald insists 'I want you to understand that I didn't install her there so that I could make love to her' as he tries to offer suggestions that he took responsibility for Eva and her situation. Cynical as it may be, offering the suggestion that he 'didn't install her' so he could 'make love to her' allows an audience to recognise that is exactly what he did do. Just like Eric, Gerald notes Eva's 'pretty' presentation and ensures that, as the dominant male with social standing in this relationship, he gains from the agreement just as much as she does, if not more as he is not reliant on her. Gerald also attempts to make the Birlings feel sorry for Eva and characterises himself as the 'fairy prince' as he 'became at once the most important person in her life'. It is this superlative phrase of 'most important' that is significant here as if he had recognised himself to hold this role, then he also should have recognised that he had the responsibility to take care of Eva which, sadly, he did not do as 'the girl's dead'. Whilst Eric's treatment of Eva is slightly different to Gerald's in that he 'insisted on giving her enough money to keep her going', he again only pays attention to her financial needs as this is what society, most notably his father, has taught him to do throughout his life. Eric fails to recognise that Eva would have needed him to take responsibility for her emotions as more than just 'a thing'. This is a need that Eric must understand as he scorns his father for 'not [being] the kind of father a chap could go to when he's in trouble'. What this suggests is that Eric understands that those who can must take responsibility not only for others' financial wellbeing but also for their emotional wellbeing. Having not been shown this himself, he fails to show it to others. It is only when his own sister begins to acknowledge the part that she played in Eva's death that he begins to learn from her as an 'impressionable' young man.

Whilst the women of the play with higher social standings do not necessarily use Eva for their own gain, they use their power in order to ensure that she is unable to take responsibility for herself. Eva is rendered a voiceless character as a result of her 'suicide, of course' yet even before she meets her untimely death, she is unable to advocate for herself in Milwards and is deemed not to be a 'deserving case' by Mrs Birling. It is at this point that we, as an audience, begin to question the nature of the adjective 'deserving'. In a socialist environment, Eva surely is the manifestation of 'deserving'. She is 'alone, friendless, almost penniless, desperate' where this listing emphasises the clear need that she had for someone, anyone, to take responsibility for her and her welfare. Eva's attempts to take responsibility for herself and ask for her 'rates raised' is not a 'ridiculous air' but a basic need to thrive in society. Priestley offers us hope in the form of Eric and Sheila at the close of the play as they acknowledge that 'it's what happened to the girl and what we all did to her that matters'. The first person plural pronoun 'we' is what we must recognise here as it is not singular actions that cause disastrous consequences or, indeed, cause change. Moreover, Priestley was imploring all audiences, through the mouthpieces of his characters, to take responsibility for themselves in order to take responsibility for others, ensuring that this theme is undoubtedly one of – if not the most – important focal points of the play.

> **How has the candidate grouped their ideas together within this response?**
>
> Ideas about the writer's methods, meanings and links to the context of the play are all carefully balanced together here to present a well-rounded response.

Critical response

This response is a confident and well-developed piece of writing that deals with the main ideas of the text whilst also carefully analysing the way in which language and structural devices support the writer's intentions. The candidate understands the text in thorough detail which is demonstrated by the many references that are neatly embedded throughout. References are commented on with an assured understanding of the effect of the methods alongside terminology that is accurate and supports the analysis (it is not just included for the sake of it!) There is a mature appreciation of the play's context that is not overlooked when understanding the significance of this central theme within the text. The careful planning of the essay allows for ideas to be grouped in a sensible order that progresses in a natural style.

The use of time

3.5 How does Priestley use time to offer his message on society in *An Inspector Calls*?

3.5.1 Critical response

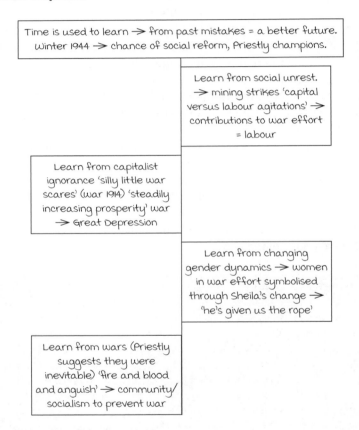

Time is used to learn → from past mistakes = a better future. Winter 1944 → chance of social reform, Priestly champions.

Learn from social unrest. → mining strikes 'capital versus labour agitations' → contributions to war effort = labour

Learn from capitalist ignorance 'silly little war scares' (war 1914) 'steadily increasing prosperity' war → Great Depression

Learn from changing gender dynamics → women in war effort symbolised through Sheila's change → 'he's given us the rope'

Learn from wars (Priestly suggests they were inevitable) 'fire and blood and anguish' → community/ socialism to prevent war

Starting with context is a convincing way to respond to this question. The candidate's knowledge of the text's social and political context forms a strong and confident opening paragraph.

Whilst many focus on the first performance of *An Inspector Calls* in the Soviet Union, examining how time influences the play actually begins in Priestley's original writing of the play in the winter of 1944. Whilst the allied victory may have been assumed by this point, Britain was still in a time of war when Priestley devised his concept. It is in this time of uncertainty and complex politics that Priestley created a play almost antithetical to this time: a simple play, with a clear message. Priestley sets the events of *An Inspector Calls* in 1912 to force the audience to learn from their mistakes. Performed in a post-war era, the audience might view the Birling family as incredibly distanced from their own reality; the truth was that Britain was on a precipice at that moment, and they could head towards a changed society, or return to the behaviours of the Birlings, and the wider public, in 1912.

Our first opportunity to learn from the mistakes of 1912 presents in Priestley highlighting the agitations surrounding the labour market in the pre-war years. We are encouraged to learn from the social unrest of 1912 and the potential impacts of this in the following years. Birling calls them 'capital versus labour agitations' and believes that by 1940 all the unrest will be 'forgotten'. Arguably, we could consider this correct – both periods of war take away elements of social unrest as various areas of the country focus their time on the war effort. Indeed, the rationing of WWII in many ways dissolves the divide between the employers and the employees, a divide Birling seems all too aware of, with the juxtaposition between 'capital' and 'labour' exemplifying a divide in social class, not just where people work. The perhaps belittling noun of 'agitations' represents Mr Birling's desire to ignore any labour disruption, despite the miner strike of 1912 involving over one million people. Mr Birling's ignorance is something that the audience should learn from: key strikes continued in 1919, 1921, and then the General Strike of 1926 that involved over 1.5 million workers. Mr Birling's confident tone asserts that this disruption will end, when in fact it only increased, even continuing in WWII. Priestley wants his audience to learn from Mr Birling's mistakes. His arrogance and ignorance lead to his belief that money can be used to control those beneath him, in the same way that he ends his workers' strike because eventually they would need his money. Priestley is utilising the audience's knowledge of what actually happened to draw their attention to the promises that socialism, or at least the Labour Party, might offer Britain: less 'agitations' and more equality, something that had been created accidentally during WWII.

Notably, Mr Birling's ignorance continues into his understanding of wider political unrest and the global climate. He may believe that labour disruption will end and time will show he is incorrect, but Priestley also wants us to learn from the Capitalist ignorance that could not foresee the potential carnage of two world wars. Modern historians now understand that the First World War as a result of over a decade of events, but Mr Birling is unable to see beyond his own belief that the 'Germans don't want war' and calling the various events 'silly little war scares'. The almost childish adjectives 'silly' and 'little' seek to undermine the much more dramatic 'war scares' that follow in the sentence, and we can imagine this line performed in a mocking tone. What Mr Birling aims to do is reinforce his superiority and astute assessment of politics to his immediate audience – but what he is really doing is highlighting his stupidity and lack of awareness. Priestley criticises individuals like Mr Birling who not only ignored the signs of war but also actively discouraged any discourse

> **How does the candidate show a strong understanding of both when the play was written and when it was set?**

> There is convincing exploration of both tone and word choice here, tying the analysis in to the overall argument.

> **How does the candidate constantly return to the impact on the audience in this response?**

> This response has a strong awareness of the dramatic form, both with its discussion over tone and its consideration here of staging.

How does this opening idea link back to the introduction?

The analysis here is embedded well into the general response. The exploration of effect builds on the overall idea discussed.

How does the candidate clearly return to the question at this point?

The judicious use of subject terminology here makes for a sophisticated comment on Priestley's use of language.

around what could happen. This reluctance to view the world beyond their own dining room is often presented in stage versions where the Birlings remain within the confines of their home, unable to view the world beyond their doorstep.

This precipice moment for post-war Britain is not only highlighted in what they can learn from war and labour agitations, but also in what they can learn about gender following the war period. Both world wars changed the role of women in society, and Priestley highlights some of these changes through the change occurring in Sheila throughout the play. In many ways, Sheila experiences an epiphany through the influence of the Inspector, as she breaks away from the various male influences society places on her. Arguably, her understanding of the Inspector is far more astute than her father's, as she tells the others 'he's given us the rope – so that we'll hang ourselves'. This metaphor, perhaps representative of the social suicide the Birlings must accept in order to gain a sense of redemption, emphasises Sheila's intellect as she shows an inherent ability to read the events of the evening in a way the other cannot. Her decision to not take the ring back from Gerald is symbolic of her rejection of male oppression and may encourage the audience to learn from this newly independent woman, an uncommon feature of society in 1945, let alone in 1912. In many ways, women returned to their traditional role in the household following WWII, so Priestley's attempt to engage the audience in this change perhaps was unsuccessful. What the war and the role of Sheila can exemplify is how a woman's horizons can be broadened beyond the limits that societal expectations place on her. Priestley's audience is forced to consider how Sheila will not allow these limits to be placed on her and, with the feminist movement in the 1960s, perhaps Priestley was in some ways ahead of his time in this social message.

The destruction and chaos caused by both world wars, and what we must learn from them, is how Priestley utilises time in the closing act. Priestley, through his mouthpiece of the Inspector, warns against the 'fire and blood and anguish' that will occur if people do not learn and change. The polysyndeton encourages the actor to pause before each bleak noun, each representing the carnage that will be brought about by war. Priestley draws a direct correlation here between the selfish actions of the Birlings (and therefore the upper class as a whole) and the world wars that follow. Birling's earlier belittling of the wars shows his ignorance that they will occur, but Priestley again plays on time to tell the audience that the wars are a 'lesson' that humanity will be 'taught'. Priestley encourages his audience to learn from this moment, and indeed the death and suffering that occurred between 1912 and 1945. Throughout the play, Priestley is constantly using the Birling family in 1912 to highlight what the audience need to learn and, in this way, the play is actually rather simple. Get rid of the ignorance, unrest and various divides that, in reality, still occur in society and use the end of World War Two to improve the way the public behave and interact, following a time of extreme upheaval. In the following election and the shifts that happened post-war, perhaps many of Priestley's didactic criticisms were valid and did ignite change.

These final comments summarise the key ideas argued throughout the response.

Critical response

This answer is critical, particularly with its understanding of the interrelationship between text and context. The comments on the social, political and historical influences that encouraged Priestley are used to explore how time is used by the playwright, showing an excellent understanding of the text as a construct. This drives the answer and the analytical comments are integrated well into these ideas. The excellent selection of evidence shows a thorough understanding of the play whilst consistently justifying their ideas.

Eva Smith as the most significant character

3.6 To what extent could it be suggested that Eva Smith is arguably the most significant character in the play despite her remaining voiceless?

3.6.1 Critical response

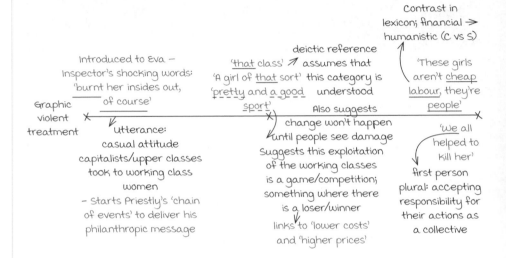

Graphic violent treatment

Introduced to Eva – Inspector's shocking words: 'burnt her insides out, of course'

Utterance: casual attitude capitalists/upper classes took to working class women – Starts Priestly's 'chain of events' to deliver his philanthropic message

deictic reference 'that class' assumes that this category is understood

'A girl of that sort' 'pretty and a good sport'

Also suggests change won't happen until people see damage Suggests this exploitation of the working classes is a game/competition; something where there is a loser/winner links to 'lower costs' and 'higher prices'

Contrast in lexicon; financial → humanistic (C vs S)

'These girls aren't cheap labour, they're people'

'We all helped to kill her'

first person plural: accepting responsibility for their actions as a collective

This opening illustrates the candidate's response to the task whilst also acknowledging the significance of contextual awareness. The writer's intentions and decisions are clearly acknowledged.

Ostensibly, Eva Smith may appear to be a voiceless pawn in Priestley's political diatribe, yet on closer inspection, it is only through being exposed to the suffering that Eva faces, projected through the characters' confessions, that any change can be dreamed of being facilitated at all. In fact, Eva's physical absence from the play mirrors the way in which many of the more privileged members of society would have viewed 'girls of [her] sort' within the Britain of 1912 – invisible. Through the characters, most notably the Inspector, Priestley gifts Eva a voice. Her tale is heard by the audience and it is the different voices that help to narrate the tale that also allows the audience to understand the stark contrasts between the capitalist and socialist views of the time. Primarily through Inspector Goole, our attention is drawn to Eva's story as we begin to understand a sense of her humanity, what she stood for and, tragically, how her life met its untimely demise.

Eva's legacy is present within the play almost as soon as the Inspector enters the Birlings' home. There are no formal niceties to her introduction to the family and, instead, the Inspector introduces her as 'a young woman'. Interestingly, the presentation of Eva here by the Inspector is hugely different to the Birlings' acknowledgement of her as a 'girl'. Whilst this might not immediately seem concerning, this subtle difference in the way the two parties refer to her speaks volumes about the way in which they treat her. The noun 'woman' holds connotations of an older female, someone who is in control of themselves and has grown up beyond her youth. This noun's counterpart 'girl' suggests one who is, in terms of age, much younger. A girl is often considered to be a woman who has not reached maturity. A younger age is frequently associated with being considered inferior to an elder. It is this view of Eva that continues to permeate the dramatic action. The Birlings viewed Eva as an immature female who they felt was inferior to them thus rendering her at their will and whim.

The Inspector continues to flesh out Eva's tragic death as he explains that she had 'swallowed a lot of strong disinfectant. Burnt her insides out, of course' before adding that this death was 'Suicide of course'. The repetition of the adverbial phrase 'of course' here is what becomes interesting on closer inspection. The Inspector's graphic yet casual revelation of how Eva Smith died could serve to show how common deaths like this were in the early 20th century; it could also be intended to draw polarisation between how the Inspector responds to this death when compared to how the Birlings react. Mr Birling merely responds that it is 'horrible business' and attempts to move the conversation forward, yet the Inspector is stuck on the image of Eva's death. After all, his whole character as a device relies on his occupancy with the death of Eva Smith. It is the second utterance of 'of course' that begins to really garner attention. This second phrase feels almost satirical as suicide was punished as a crime in England and Wales until 1961. Yet, more than this, the crime of suicide was condemned as a mortal sin in the eyes of the Church. Does the Inspector telling the Birlings that her death was 'suicide' play into their view that all working class women were sinners? Does his assertion of this category of death attempt to show the ridiculous nature of holding such a view when it is a young woman – a real, living person with who the Birlings came into physical contact – who died? Not only could Priestley be attempting to change the Birlings', and those who are represented by them, views on 'community' and the working class, but it may also show Priestley trying to shift public attitudes towards not only suicide but also many other things in line with the secularisation of society that sought to treat people as just that, people.

Arguably, in a play where the primary theme is considered to be social class, the relationship that Mrs Birling has with Eva Smith is interesting. Through this relationship, Priestley brings the issue of gender discrimination into sharp focus, using the focalisation of Sybil. The opening stage directions highlight the fact that Mrs Sybil Birling is her 'husband's social superior' which, whilst

Can you identify how the candidate uses subtle references to make larger, whole text comments?

The development of ideas is built carefully through a precise focus on individual moments and ideas.

How are multiple meanings discussed here? Why does this make the response successful?

There is a confident and perceptive tone that is presented here when discussing the impact of context on the content. Insightful suggestions are drawn that contribute to the candidate's overall argument.

How does the candidate use subject terminology to elevate their response here?

initially surprising, may not draw too much attention in terms of the progression of the plot. The Birlings' whole social construction is built on the pride that they place on their position in society, yet it was often much more common to see the practice of hypergamy where a marriage occurred between two people of unequal social class positions. As such, Mrs Birling's hypogamy may well contribute to her acute awareness of social class, which she then uses as a weapon towards Eva Smith. By marrying someone of a lower class than herself, Mrs Birling would be well aware of how her marital position impacted her social status and we are offered no reasons for this happening in the Birlings' marriage. Within act 2, Mrs Birling refers to Eva as one of the 'girls of that class–' before being stopped by her daughter. Again, towards the end of the act, she remarks 'as if a girl of that sort would ever refuse money'. Specifically, the use of the deictic reference 'that' in both statements suggests the audience, and those with whom Mrs Birling addresses on stage, assume a position of shared understanding with her of what 'that class' or 'that sort' means as she never quantifies this statement. What we do understand, however, is that this deictic reference is used pejoratively here. Further supporting Sybil's scathing assertions of Eva is her use of the noun 'sort' when attempting to describe Eva purely as a result of her social class. A 'sort' is a classification term, but by not specifically using the term 'class' here, like Sybil did the first time that she tried to identify Eva by her 'class' alone, she further renders the class that Eva belongs to as not even worthy of being referred to as belonging to a social class. So, for a woman who is so aware of her own position in society as a result of her hypogamic marriage, Sybil's attempt to render Eva Smith as less than could be an attempt to assert her own status in society further. The Inspector warns Mrs Birling that she is 'making it worse for herself', which could be the Inspector's way of warning Sybil that she is villainising herself further by attempting to widen the gulf between herself and Eva Smith. This allows the audience to understand Priestley's powerful message here that social class and gender are not reasons for not supporting the 'community'. Attempting to elevate your own status by diminishing someone else's only serves to ensure that your behaviour will be judged harshly before you are 'taught' a serious 'lesson'.

In a society where there are those who win and those who lose, Eric's assertion that Eva was 'pretty and a good sport', which he attempts to use as a reason for his casual sexual interaction with her, quite hauntingly highlights this. Initially, Eric notices how Eva looks; she is 'pretty', something that his sister opposingly disliked her for. This, again, reinforces the struggle that young women who found themselves in poverty had to live with. Whilst her attractiveness enabled her to potentially seek work in the Palace Bar – 'a haunt of women of the town' – it also led to her losing her respectable employment at Milwards through another woman's jealousy. It seems as if poverty is a game that no one could win. Eric also dehumanises Eva when he metaphorically refers to her as a 'good sport'.

Within sport, there is competition and an element of triumph for one party. Whilst Eric ostensibly wins in his attempt to have relations with her, ultimately Eva wins – not for herself, but for what she represents within the play. It is Eva's story that is heard and it is Eric and Sheila's views of her and all 'girls of [her] class' that change by the close of the curtain.

Eva's legacy and message are clear at the end of the play. Whilst Sheila understands the magnitude of her own actions towards Eva quite early on in the play (where she insists that 'these girls aren't cheap labour, they're people', after the Inspector states that 'each of you helped to kill her'), Eric's outburst that 'the girl's dead and we all helped to kill her' solidifies the change in the younger generation that Priestley wished to see ripple through his audiences for long to come. Eric's use of the first person plural pronoun 'we' clearly highlights that he doesn't take singular responsibility for her death, but acknowledges that all of his family, Gerald, and audiences are responsible for the treatment of 'millions and millions and millions' of girls' deaths like this as long as social inequality and poverty permeate society's landscape. And so, for as long as the character of Eva Smith continues to represent more than one girl and is symbolic of all those who find themselves in desolate situations, she will remain the most significant character in the play. It is her death and her treatment that set off the whole 'chain of events' that we see unfold on stage right before our very eyes.

A confident response relies on a confident understanding of the play. Identify all of the references that are used throughout this response to highlight textual security.

By directly referring to the task in the closing paragraph, the candidate carefully rounds off their argument.

Critical response

Whilst this essay title may have resulted in a response that focused on the one character of Eva Smith, this candidate has shown their developed understanding of the play as they successfully explore the relationships of multiple characters to the named one of the task. Links between the characters, context and themes and probed carefully and rely on the candidate's developed understanding of the text as a construct. References are judiciously selected and we witness the candidate's ability to move from the specific to the general with ease. A critical writing style is established as the candidate analytically explores the main ideas of the play in a conceptual way. There is no doubt that the candidate has a secure awareness of the relationship between language, structure and form and these elements are explored perceptively with terminology used to enhance the response.

Comparative poetry

The effects of war

4.1 Compare how poets present the effects of war in *Bayonet Charge* by Ted Hughes and one other poem.

4.1.1 Clear response

meaning and ideas	Structure and language
Heat and pressure of war; an intense environment Hot = running, explosions, nerves Leads to molten iron chest = patriotism	Touchy dynamite = metaphor Could explode 'touchy' No more emotion = war destroys humanity
Compare openings of each poem 'suddenly he awoke and was running' 'our brains ache' Individual vs collective effects of war — but both represent all?	Compare use of rhetorical questions for questioning purpose of war 'what are we doing here?' 'in what cold clockwork'

The candidate begins by effectively using references to support their interpretation.

How might the ideas here be developed with a comment on the poem's structure?

Does the candidate join their ideas together, or are they offering separated, isolated ideas? How might they create a more cohesive essay?

One of the consequences of war is dealing with the intense heat and pressure that it creates. For the speaker in *Bayonet Charge*, he is 'running/raw in raw-seamed hot khaki'. The repetition of raw strongly conveys the way the soldier feels, as the adjective 'raw' can suggest someone is in pain. Furthermore, this adds to a semantic field of heat in the first stanza with 'hot', 'sweating' and 'molten', highlighting the intense pressure the soldier is under. He might be hot because of running, the explosions around him, or perhaps the feeling of nervousness from having to run into inevitable death. Hughes might want to show his readers the reality of war: it is a high-pressure environment and this affects soldiers both mentally and physically.

Through the poem, we find that another effect of war is a loss of emotion or humanity. By the end of the poem, he has become 'touchy dynamite'. This metaphor hints to us that the soldier is losing what makes him human, like his emotions and his purpose to fight. The adjective 'touchy' suggests that war is so difficult that he might go off at any minute like a human explosive. Hughes is encouraging the reader to sympathise with soldiers who begin to feel that there is no point in feeling emotion when at war.

Whilst Hughes presents an individual's experience of war and how it affects him, Wilfred Owen seems to be sharing the voice of all soldiers and the effects on them in his poem *Exposure*. Hughes opens the poem with 'Suddenly he awoke and was running' whereas Owen begins with 'Our brains ache in the merciless iced east winds'. Both poems tell us immediately who is involved in the war and how they are affected by it. The adverb 'suddenly' suggests to us that events in war can happen without any notice and the soldier must be prepared. It is clear he is alone with the pronoun 'he' so Hughes is telling us the experience of one individual. For Owen, however, the effect he focuses on is not the suddenness of war but the sense of mental pain with the verb 'ache'. The use of first person plural immediately tells the reader that Owen is commenting on all soldiers' experiences and sharing how they are impacted collectively. Owen wants to tell the WWI readers that soldiers had to rely on each other to deal with the impact of war, whereas Hughes decides to share how one individual mind can be affected – either way they tell the reader about how war is far more sudden and mentally painful than the reader might realise.

> The analytical comments here support the response. They consider how meaning and effects are created through the ways both poems begin.

In both *Bayonet Charge* and *Exposure*, the soldiers are affected by war because they lose their patriotism or reason to fight. In *Bayonet Charge*, he loses 'the patriotic tear that had brimmed in his eye' and in *Exposure* they start to realise that even though people are dying 'nothing happens'. The use of personification in *Bayonet Charge* reveals that he is losing his purpose because the patriotism is leaving his body in the tears. On the other hand, Owen uses repetition to constantly remind the reader that nothing happens or changes in war. This affects the soldiers as they lose all hope of being helped and protected from the harsh weather conditions. Perhaps both poets offer a similar, negative message on war. They want to educate the reader and help them understand that a soldier may enter a war for the right reasons, but it does not take long for war to affect them mentally and take that away.

> **Could the candidate develop their ideas about patriotism here? There is a good opportunity to explore, in detail, how war impacts patriotism – how might this be improved?**

> **Clear response**
> This response is clear in its response to the question and the comparative comments are clear. It is not yet a thoughtful response as the ideas appear disjointed, and at times, lack detail and depth. The comparison paragraphs are stronger, whereas the paragraphs on *Bayonet Charge* alone need more development.

4.1.2 Thoughtful response

Owen's *Exposure* and Hughes' *Bayonet Charge* create detailed imagery of the landscape of war and the effect it has on the men that fight. Both poems also consider the role nature must play within conflict.

> This introduction attempts to set out an overall response to the question.

In *Bayonet Charge*, Hughes describes war as a high-pressured and intense environment that appears to have no escape. Throughout the first stanza, war is described as a heat-filled landscape where the soldier is placed under extreme pressure and has no choice but to run, despite his 'hot khaki' feeling 'raw' and the 'sweating [...] molten' tear falling from his chest. This semantic field immediately establishes not only how the soldier's immediate running has caused him to sweat and his uniform to rub, but also the pain and intensity

> **The candidate mentions this semantic field being in the first stanza. Could this be developed into a structural comment?**

> The response becomes more detailed here and shows good understanding of the poem's main ideas.

of running across no man's land, perhaps revealing the nerves and anxiety the soldier feels. This emotional reaction, therefore, can link to the idea of 'raw' emotions. The repetition of the adjective 'raw' to describe both him and his uniform ('raw in raw-seamed hot khaki') forces the reader to imagine the hot landscape (unlike the cold but equally painful and intense landscape of *Exposure*) as reflective of the soldier's inner struggles. Despite this, he continues running, and here Hughes tells us of the devastating reality of war. It has the effect of almost making the soldier 'numb', as despite the 'raw' and 'hot' environment, he continues running because he must – as do all soldiers who have no choice in what they must face.

> The response to this question becomes more cohesive as this second paragraph builds on the ideas of the first (focusing on the way the soldier has become numb).

This numb reaction is exacerbated in the closing lines of the poem where the soldier ultimately becomes an object. In the final line, we are told of 'his terror's touchy dynamite', and we can interpret this as the soldier's ultimate sacrifice to his cause, as he loses his purpose and becomes a weapon of war. The metaphor of 'dynamite' is interesting as it establishes the soldier as a mere mindless explosive, indicating that his loss of patriotism and purpose has resulted in him losing his humanity (whereas the soldiers in *Exposure* simply lose their purpose and suffer the consequences). He is also 'touchy', suggesting that the intense pressure of war has left him unstable, like a bomb that might go off at any minute. So, whilst he may serve his purpose and keep running on his charge, his inability to think rationally may tell us that he is now unable to fight or sense danger, and he is now 'touchy' and ready to explode or die. So, Hughes gives us an interesting effect of war, the idea that it takes away an individual's humanity, and leaves them as simply a weapon.

> **Could this idea about Hughes' message consider the specific context of the poem and Hughes himself?**

Both Owen and Hughes begin their poems by taking us straight into the trauma and pain of war. Hughes begins with 'suddenly he awoke and was running' and Owen tells us 'our brains ache'. This immediate placing us into the action puts both speakers and readers into the horrifying and intense landscape of war, telling us of the impact on either the group or the individual. Whilst Owen presents us with a sense of unity immediately, with the plural pronoun 'our' allowing the reader to envisage a group suffering and 'ach[ing]' in war, Hughes focuses on the single soldier and his journey. However, because his soldier is anonymous, we sense that he represents all soldiers completing their charge, and then both poems offer us a universal version of the effects of war. Owen and Hughes both highlight the pain and trauma, whether it is the physical pain or the emotional impact, where each soldier begins to question why they carry on in a world of suffering.

> This first comparison considers how each poem begins, offering thoughtful and developed comparison between the two poems. This is sustained throughout the rest of the essay.

Both speakers seem to question their participation or place in war, although, neither seems to use this question to exact an actual change. This questioning of war and purpose becomes a crucial effect of war; significantly, both poets use rhetorical questions to highlight the concerns of each speaker. In *Exposure*,

> There are apt, well-chosen references here which are integrated well into the paragraph and show secure knowledge of the chosen poem.

there are multiple questions finishing stanzas, such as 'is it that we are dying?' and 'what are we doing here?', whilst in *Bayonet Charge* he asks, 'in what cold clockwork of the stars [...] was he the hand pointing that second?'. These questions point the readers towards a feeling of confusion and uncertainty, and both poets remind us that nothing is certain in war. For Owen, however, the questions are far blunter and explore the futility of conflict itself, with 'what are we doing here?' directly targeting the officers and generals who lead their men to slaughter, a personal experience of Owen's and a trauma he had to suffer himself. Whereas Hughes' speaker questions the universe itself, asking why the fate in the 'stars' has made him the soldier fighting at that moment. Critically, both speakers are questioning their circumstances: why me? Hughes and Owen leave us thinking that war, therefore, strips its soldiers of patriotism and purpose, and leaves them questioning their own position in war, and we are left, as readers, questioning war itself.

> **Again, could the candidate link to the context of when each poet was writing to draw out a more detailed comparison here?**

> **Thoughtful response**
> This essay moves to thoughtful, particularly for the AO1 criteria. It offers a detailed and clever comparison of the two poems, pulling them together closely by considering both structural and language choices that link well. The quotations fully support the interpretation and the writer's choices are examined closely.

4.1.3 Critical response

Both Hughes and Owen present war as an endless mental battle, one that the soldiers will inevitably lose. It is clear that they are attempting to educate the reader on the loss of humanity that conflict causes.

> By focusing on the mental rather than physical effects of war, the candidate has created more opportunities for conceptual exploration.

Losing his purpose and patriotism, Hughes' speaker faces an internal battle that destroys his motivation to survive. As the poem progresses, he is so affected by war that he dismisses his reasons as 'king, honour, human dignity etcetera/ Dropped like luxuries'. Evidently, Hughes offers the reader the true impact of war: a gradual loss of humanity. Through losing his purpose, the speaker loses his basic human instincts and is no longer able to make the decision between fight and flight – a seriously dangerous position for a soldier to be in. He perceives his purpose to now be mere 'luxuries' – the simile here highlights how war causes an individual to dismiss anything which can be a 'luxur[y]' – but, of course, the reader knows that his motivation should not be something he can dismiss and 'drop', instead something he should protect for its value. Furthermore, the asyndetic listing makes each purpose become less significant, establishing a dismissive tone and highlighting the distance the speaker creates between himself and his purpose. Hughes reinforces to the reader that morale and motivation is irrelevant in moments of conflict; humans most go back to the basic fight or flight instincts to survive.

> There is a mature analysis of language here, where subject terminology is precise and the meanings created are explored in a concise way.

> **How has this response started to have an overall thread?**

How are references used successfully in this paragraph? How are they skilfully interwoven into the candidate's ideas?

The opening idea of war being a mental battle that the soldiers will lose is further developed throughout this paragraph.

There is a sustained and exploratory comparison here of the meaning and ideas within each poem, rather than moving to analytical comments.

How can we consider this a successful exploration of the purpose, and context, of each poem?

The candidate's ideas become perceptive here and the comparison of methods allows them to make specific and clever comparisons.

The candidate shows precise understanding of how specific words and devices create various meanings.

Hughes wishes to emphasise the loss of humanity by presenting the soldier's transition to a weapon of war. In the final line of the poem, we learn that the soldier is now 'touchy dynamite'. Structurally, Hughes leaves us with this final line, forcing us to question the soldier's fate. At this point, his death seems inevitable, written in the 'cold clockwork of the stars' and yet, this final use of chremamorphism draws our attention to the ultimate outcome of conflict – a loss of compassion, motivation, indeed, humanity – as the soldier becomes an object of war. Hughes' use of chremamorphism is key as it removes the emotion from the soldier, and allows him to be a weapon, his only function now is to explode and join the conflict. This, paired with the adjective 'touchy', hints at the speaker's state of intense pressure, building from the 'raw' 'heat' at the opening of the poem to now becoming an explosive in the pressure cooker of war. Undeniably, Hughes is enforcing his view that soldiers are mere weapons of those in charge – the mental impact of war is insignificant if he fulfils the soldier's destiny, to enter his 'charge' and sacrifice himself for his country. This is a battle that he will inevitably lose.

Both *Exposure* and *Bayonet Charge* explore the various mental impacts of war and how soldiers no longer have the mental capacity to process anything but pain. The war faced by the soldiers in each poem is different. Whilst in *Exposure*, Owen offers two enemies, Hughes' speaker barely mentions the enemy he faces. Instead, he alludes to the various weaponry of war and the clumsy movements of the soldier, as he sees the 'green hedge that dazzled with rifle fire'. Indeed, Hughes leaves the enemy as a vague entity, whereas Owen's enemies are clear, is it the 'pale flakes with fingering stealth' that his soldiers fear – of course, there are bullets, but they are 'less deadly than the snow'. Despite these varying enemies, the impact remains the same. Both poems offer soldiers mentally impacted by their experiences. It is the relentless nature of the war – whether it be weather or a human enemy – that affects them. Both poets may be calling for a review of the mental injuries of war, interesting when we consider their early to mid-20th century publishing dates, a time when mental injuries were little understood. Perhaps this is what concerns both Hughes and Owen.

Both poets unpick the conflict between nature and warfare in their poems. For Owen, he emphasises in the opening lines how 'our brains ache, in the merciless iced east winds that knife us', whereas Hughes reveals how the 'bullets' are 'smacking the belly out of the air'. Notably, each poet utilises personification here, but both offer starkly contrasting ideas. For Owen, it is the weather that is personified as 'merciless' and, therefore, relentless in its attack on the soldiers – even in the opening line. The violent verb to 'knife' the soldiers reinforces this sense of aggression from the weather and, therefore, establishes how the soldiers are slowly losing their humanity, as they desperately attempt to face an attack from something that surrounds them that they can't fight back against. Conversely, Hughes' use of personification highlights the danger of warfare rather than the weather. In fact, Hughes' personification presents the weather, the very air, as vulnerable, with the violent verb 'smacking' here describing the bullets, unlike Owen's violent verb describing nature. So, whilst both poets use personification, it offers a very different impact on the reader. Furthermore, the poems contrasting use of pronouns further establish the impact of war, with Owen's opening line engineering a sense of unity and togetherness, with the first person plural pronouns 'our' and 'us' used to begin and end the opening line, offering an immediate sense of a bonded group of men, who not only share the experience of war but also the trauma of it too, unlike the singular figure of *Bayonet Charge* who has to suffer alone.

How does the analysis become fine-grained and insightful? How does the candidate explore the methods used by both poets?

Critical response

This response approaches the question of effects of war with a conceptual focus, considering the mental battle and inevitable loss the soldiers face. In doing so, the candidate ensures their analytical comments strengthen this overall response. The comparison becomes precise and is interwoven and the final two paragraphs have a real balance of ideas between the two poems. The essay also considers various contextual implications, such as the time of writing, as well as exploring the concepts and ideas that relate to the task given.

The power of nature

4.2 Compare how the power of the natural world is presented in *The Prelude* by William Wordsworth and one other poem.

4.2.1 Clear response

The natural world (nw) is powerful more powerful than humans realise	Humans recognise the power of nw and sit by and watch and wait	Both poems show that the power of the nw is not fully understood and leaves the speaker unclear
'Huge peak black and huge' 'upreared its head' 'troubled pleasure'	'we are prepared' 'spits like a tame cat turned savage'	
'was a trouble to my dreams'	'It is a huge nothing that we fear'	

The candidate begins by showing an understanding of the context of *The Prelude* before then linking the main ideas to the second poem. The ideas are clearly linked.

Within *The Prelude*, Wordsworth's speaker (often thought to be a young Wordsworth himself as the poem is autobiographical) explores what can happen when the natural world is disturbed by humans. A similar idea is presented within *Storm on the Island* where it is nature that takes over the island and the islanders find themselves powerless to stop it or protect themselves from it. Both poems, therefore, show the impact that the natural world can have on humans and explore the idea that humans do not fully understand the devastating effect that the natural world can have on people.

This first paragraph only touches upon one idea with an attempt to comment on language. How could this idea be extended and developed?

As the young boy rows out into the lake, there is a sense that he knows he should not be doing this as this action is described using the oxymoron 'troubled pleasure'. Whilst the young boy gets 'pleasure' from rowing in the stolen boat in the moonlit lake, he cannot fully enjoy this experience. The adjective 'troubled' suggests that, deep down, he knows that he is doing something wrong and so he cannot allow himself to fully enjoy it.

The candidate here shows an awareness of the structure of the poem. This is then clearly linked to some language analysis with well-embedded quotations. The candidate considers Wordsworth's intentions.

The poem begins to reach its climax as the mountains appear to frighten the young boy and he imagines that he sees a 'huge peak black and huge' that 'upreared its head'. Firstly, we can understand that the boy cannot fully explain what he is seeing as he repeats the adjective 'huge' twice. The effect of this is that it shows a reader that he does not have any other words to describe what he sees, but the idea of it being 'huge' could suggest that he is overwhelmed by it. Secondly, Wordsworth uses zoomorphism here to make the mountains sound like an animal who raises its head from sleeping. When animals are ready to attack or are disturbed, they can be seen to 'uprear' their heads as they prepare to defend themselves. This could show that the natural world is having to fight back against the small boy who rows on the lake uninvited. It could be Wordsworth's way of showing the reader that crimes will not go unpunished as we know that the boat was stolen in the first place.

In comparison to this, Seamus Heaney shows that the islanders in *Storm on the Island* understand how powerful the natural world can be and so they respect its power and fear it much more than the boy in *The Prelude*. Heaney starts the poem with the line 'we are prepared'. Straight away, a reader can notice the pronoun 'we', a collective, which shows that all the islanders must get ready for the storm, which represents nature's power. The verb 'prepared' also suggests that the islanders must get ready for the storm. In preparing for something, you draw on prior experience and know what to expect, suggesting that they may have been caught out by the power of the natural world before.

> There is an attempt to compare here. How could the comparison be tightened up to show a clearer understanding?

Animalistic imagery is also used by Heaney to convey nature's power. The sea is described by Heaney: 'spits like a tame cat turned savage'. The simile here is an image that all readers can understand as a 'tame cat' will often be a family pet that can be stroked and is a companion, but this simile shows that the sea, like the cat, has a temper that can change quickly. The juxtaposition of 'tame' and 'savage' reveals that the sea will always be around the island but that it can quickly become dangerous and wild, showing that the islanders understand that the sea's power could overwhelm them at any time.

> A clear thread has started to be established as the candidate specifically links images by their content, **could this link be made more explicit?**

Both poems show that the characters within the poems must live with the effects of nature's power. Within *The Prelude*, the poem ends with the line 'it was a trouble to my dreams', which reveals that even his 'dreams' that should be pleasant are disturbed by images of what he has seen as they cause him 'trouble'. As this line is at the end of the poem, it shows how much the boy has been affected by his actions because, at the start, he felt that nature 'led' him to the boat. The ending of *Storm on the Island* expresses similar ideas as the speaker admits 'it is a huge nothing that we fear', revealing that the islanders cannot name specifically what they are fearful of, but they started the poem preparing for nature to bring them a storm. Heaney shows that, like Wordsworth, the impact that the natural world has on humans is 'huge', but they both cannot be specific about exactly what it is that humans need to fear, which just adds to the power of the natural world; its exact power cannot even be named.

> The response ends by linking the two poems together. The poets' ideas are compared in order to finalise the candidate's overall ideas expressed within the response.

Clear response

This essay is a clear response to the question as the candidate deals with the power that the natural world holds and how this is expressed by the two poets. There is good use of quotations throughout, which are analysed to clarify how the power of the natural world is shown. Whilst there is a clear understanding of how the poems have similar ideas, these would need to be more closely explored and developed to produce a more thoughtful response as, at times, the ideas do not seem to be connected to the overall view and ideas.

4.2.2 Thoughtful response

This is a confident opening statement that responds to the question.

The candidate uses the adverb 'similarly', is this a close enough link to compare?

This link to the Romantic genre shows a candidate's awareness of context. Is this idea fully developed?

The candidate here attempts to engage with more complex ideas. **How could these ideas be fully explored whilst ensuring that the response is still focused on the question?**

The language analysis here builds well as the candidate confidently explores one of the poem's main images. Terminology is used well to support the ideas.

For centuries, poets have explored the ongoing battle between the human world and the natural world and the ways in which the two can live in both states of peace and conflict. Within *The Prelude*, Wordsworth explores the way in which the natural world can almost be seen to seek revenge when a human act of transgression occurs. Similarly, within *Storm on the Island*, Seamus Heaney projects an image that depicts the literal calm before the storm and how the two worlds can both collide and co-exist.

Within *The Prelude*, Wordsworth, in line with much of the fashions of the Romantic poets, personifies nature, stating that the speaker was 'led by her'. This genderised personification interestingly offers us two ideas. Firstly, it could suggest that females are given power in the natural world (depicting another battle in the human world at the time for gender equality and more recognition of women), yet potentially, Wordsworth may be suggesting that humans wrongly blame the natural world for their own mistakes. The verb 'led' could suggest that nature guided the speaker yet in a contrast to the way the Romantics commonly viewed nature's power, this is not shown to yield positive results.

Significantly, it is difficult to ascertain whether it is the natural world's inherent power that causes the actions of the mountain or whether Wordsworth is trying to explore the power of human imagination, or the power of the emotion of guilt. Wordsworth states that the peak of the craggy ridge 'as if with voluntary power instinct, upreared its head', where Wordsworth's use of anthropormorphism suggests that this peak appears to be something of a beast in nature. The image of the ride 'uprear[ing] its head' can also be suggestive of someone, or something who lies dormant until provoked. This could further suggest the potential of the natural world to uprise against humans should it need to exercise its power in any way.

Animalistic imagery within Heaney's poem projects the image of the sea that 'spits like a tame cat turned savage'. This simile allows Heaney to make some thoughtful points, like Wordsworth, about the innate strength of the natural world. The juxtaposed adjectives 'tame' and 'savage' are used to describe the two opposing states of the sea. A 'tame cat' is a familiar and non-threatening image, which allows a reader to recognise that, like a domestic cat, the sea is a figure that is often present, but potentially not paid much attention until provoked. The adjective 'savage' on the other hand holds connotations of being wild and feral. Significantly, if we were to consider the noun 'savage' as a descriptor of people, the long-held belief was that savages were barbarians and thus barbaric in nature. This then begins to draw distinctions between civilised people (the human world) and this savage world of nature where the natural world could be seen to be almost like a culture that is lawless and untouchable, bound by its own rules and ways of living. So, when considering the natural world in this way, a reader can become aware of its terrifying power and superiority because of its unpredictable nature.

Structurally, both poems indicate that after a period in which nature 'pummels' the human world, a sense of seeming calmness comes about. After Heaney's use of the semantic field of war where he describes the wind that 'dives' and 'strafes', the final line reads 'Strange, it is a huge nothing that we fear'. The caesura following 'strange' could almost be seen to represent a sigh of relief, or a break in the war and shows that the islanders can't seem to understand what it was that they were so worried about, describing it using the abstract noun 'nothing'. It becomes clear that this is potentially why the natural world is so powerful: once it returns to its 'tame' state' no one can remember why they just had to 'sit tight'. Notably, following the climactic episode of the 'spectacle' of the moving mountains, all that is left is a memory that 'moved slowly through the mind' later becoming a 'trouble' to the young boy's 'dreams' at night. Again, Wordsworth uses dichotomic language through 'trouble' and 'dreams' whereby a dream should not be plagued by troubling thoughts else it becomes a nightmare. This final line could serve as a reminder that whilst the current period of 'trembling' is over, it could easily re-surface when necessary and that the human world should be prepared. After all, when two worlds, that are very different, exist so closely together (shown through the continued juxtaposition) we never know when the savagery will again overcome the 'tame'.

> **How has the candidate successfully linked their ideas together in this final paragraph? Can you recognise how the candidate comments on the structure of the poems as well as the language?**

> **Thoughtful response**
> This essay moves to thoughtful, in particular for the AO2 criteria. The candidate understands the techniques that both poets use to express their ideas and uses terminology accurately to comment on effects and devices. The comparisons are pulled together by considering both the structure and language of the poems. Whilst this response appears to be fluent, it would benefit from some more succinct writing so the ideas are always well expressed.

4.2.3 Critical response

Overall, both Heaney and Wordsworth present the idea that nature can be both 'tame' and threatening and that it presents itself to humans as having two very contrasting personalities. Arguably, both poems highlight a nature that juxtaposes itself. Each natural entity offers a different kind of threat and will have a different impact, whether physical or psychological, on the speaker.

> This introduction sets up a clear comparative focus with a series of ideas that link the two poems.

In *The Prelude*, Wordsworth presents us with a very Romantic view of nature that accentuates its power and dominance in the human world. The speaker reflects on the way the mountain 'upreared its head', enabling him to understand his insignificance. Furthermore, this experience that took place on 'one summer evening' is a specific event in Wordsworth's upbringing and an experience that had a lasting impact on his view of nature. For Wordsworth, nature offers

> **How does this paragraph weave together the response and context in a seamless way?**

This opening paragraph skilfully uses a variety of evidence to justify the candidate's range of ideas about nature.

This structural comment is woven into an understanding of language, so the analysis becomes detailed and thorough.

Could any of the ideas in this paragraph be linked more specifically back to the introduction?

How could this opening sentence be more precise and specific?

The comparison comments carefully consider each poem in response to the task. The candidate begins to link more specifically back to their opening ideas.

two very contrasting images. Firstly, it is 'glittering idly', revealing it is both beautiful and tranquil. Secondly, nature has a both threatening and ominous aspect, and is presented as having a 'power instinct' where it can literally and metaphorically overpower the speaker as he rows across the lake. Towards the end of the poem, Wordsworth is in a 'grave and serious mood' – this enforces to the reader that the speaker is reflecting on his own mortality, presenting the idea that there is no comparison between man and nature. In addition, the statement that nature does 'not live like living men' establishes Wordsworth's notion that nature is everlasting and will never be destroyed, unlike the relatively short human existence.

Inherently aggressive, nature is presented as a force that humans can never defeat. A key method in presenting the contrasting sides of nature is the volta Wordsworth uses to sharply change the mood of the poem. When rowing the boat, the speaker uses the disjointed simile 'heaving through the water like a swan', and the aggressive verb 'heaving' juxtaposes with the stereotypical imagery of a graceful 'swan'. This reveals to the reader the volta that is about to occur, where nature suddenly takes control of the evening and overpowers the speaker. Additionally, Wordsworth uses personification to emphasise the unpredictability of nature. In the first line, nature is personified simply with the feminine pronoun 'her' and kindly leads Wordsworth on his journey, whereas after the volta, nature is personified as a beast-like monster with a 'grim shape' that enforces its authority over the speaker. Finally, Wordsworth uses a semantic field of overshadowing with dominant verbs such as 'upreared', 'towered' and 'growing' to indicate the increasing size of the mountain as well as the increasing power it exerts over the speaker. Crucially, the shift in mood across the poem is used by Wordsworth to emphasise nature's power over humanity.

Both *Storm on the Island* and *The Prelude* offer different ideas about nature. In *Storm on the Island*, Heaney's paradoxical ideas about nature is summarised in the vicious simile 'spits like a tame cat turned savage'. Here Heaney exposes the docile side of nature conflicting with the aggression of nature (perhaps nature's anger is exacerbated by the community's belief that they can defend against it). This contrasts significantly with the nature in *The Prelude*, where it appears beautiful rather than docile, and then becomes threatening but never actually fulfils its violent potential. This vehement side of nature in *Storm on the Island* is presented in the semantic field of martial vocabulary, where Heaney uses violent verbs such as 'pummels' 'bombarded' and 'exploding' to portray the full force of nature at its most powerful. This contrasts to *The Prelude* where nature is both threatening and cautious, as it doesn't attack the speaker, but warns him of its power without harming him. Interestingly, the speaker in *The Prelude* appears much more affected by the negative side of nature than the people in *Storm on the Island*, who are affected physically, but Wordsworth appears psychologically affected as the ominous mountain becomes a 'trouble to [his] dreams'.

Therefore, each poet wants to reveal the power and strength of nature, but they offer different effects – either way, nature is ultimately superior to humanity.

Heaney and Wordsworth want to draw the reader's attention to the unpredictability of nature. Both poems use a volta to highlight the definitive turning point where nature 'turned savage'. Notably, Heaney and Wordsworth use a form of metaphor to emphasise the change in nature; Heaney uses the simile 'spits like a tame cat' to hint that nature is both animalistic and raw, whereas Wordsworth uses the gentler personification of 'her' to indicate that nature has emotions which are controllable and human. This links back to the varying negative sides of nature, where Heaney enforces a violent and aggressive nature, whereas Wordsworth's negative nature is threatening yet controlled. This feminine personification is later transformed into an animalistic presence, much like *Storm on the Island*, when the mountain 'upreared its head', almost like a monster rising to exert its dominance over the speaker. Interestingly, both poets use oxymorons to establish how nature can be both helpful and a hindrance. In *Storm on the Island*, the sea is 'exploding comfortably', and in *The Prelude,* the speaker is in a state of 'troubled pleasure'. These immediate juxtapositions establish a contradiction for the reader where nature is, again, conflicted and confusing for the speaker. The present participle verb 'exploding' indicates the ongoing battle humanity has with nature, whilst the adjective 'troubled' reveals more about humanity's unease and wariness towards nature. Whilst *Storm on the Island* explores the power of nature more, *The Prelude* is driven by how humanity reacts to nature's power. Finally, both poets use repetition to enforce how nature can take away everything that is protective and comforting. In *Storm on the Island*, the reader is reminded that there are 'no trees, no natural shelter' and the repetition of the absolute 'no' highlights the lack of control for the people as well as the fact there are no tangible objects to keep them (and the reader) secure from the violent nature. Moreover, Wordsworth uses repetition in the closing lines of *The Prelude*, where the speaker no longer only sees the beauty of nature, there are 'no pleasant images [...] no colours' and again uses the repetition of 'no' to evoke that the 'huge peak' will always scar his memory, and though the impact of nature in *Storm on the Island* was solely physical, in *The Prelude* the psychological effects of nature's power will live on with the speaker forever.

How has evidence been used in this paragraph to support the given interpretation?

The response now becomes exploratory and critical, considering how each poet uses specific choices to develop meaning, and how these choices might link or contrast.

The response moves from general structural comparison to specific language techniques, into word comparison, with terminology integrated into this exploratory analysis.

How does the candidate successfully provide equal coverage of both poems in this final paragraph?

Critical response
This response has features of a critical essay, mainly due to the depth of analysis offered. AO2 is explored through comments about form, structure, and language, and the essay moves from the macro to the micro in terms of how it unpicks writer's methods. It provides a clear overview which links the presentation of nature in both poems, considering nature's impact on humanity and therefore offering high-level understanding of both poems.

Conflict – *The Charge of the Light Brigade*

4.3 Compare how ideas about conflict are presented in *The Charge of the Light Brigade* by Alfred, Lord Tennyson and one other poem.

4.3.1 Critical response

Conflict between people – proletariat and ruling classes. Conflict within the city.	Conflict within the army – the soldiers who 'do and die' and the leader who 'blundered', powerless to speak.
'runs in blood down palace walls'	'Forward, the Light Brigade! Charge for the guns!' he said.
'chartered street', 'chartered Thames' Conflict between the sounds of the city and the people – 'cry', sigh' 'blights with plagues the marriage hearse'	Dactylic dimeter – no let up for the soldiers. Verbs – all what they did – not what happened to them or what they said 'fought', 'plunged'...

This is a confident and critical opening to the essay. A clear link is made between these two poems that might not seem like an obvious pairing on first look, before developing a critical standpoint – oppressed voices.

How does the candidate develop their ideas successfully in this paragraph?

Blake's politically charged poem *London* ostensibly conveys the conflict between the people living within London – the proletariat and the ruling classes – however, his poem also makes a wider comment on fractured societies that fail to function effectively. This conflict between those with power and those without is also echoed within Tennyson's *The Charge of the Light Brigade* as the light brigade appear powerless to make decisions for themselves despite recognising the 'wild' commands being given by their superiors. Both poems deal with the subject of oppressed voices – those who cannot advocate for themselves, who do not have the means or facility to do so, despite potentially knowing that they need to.

The struggle between the proletariat and the ruling classes is clearly depicted through Blake's political allusion where he notes that the 'soldier's sigh runs in blood down palace walls'. Specifically, the allusion of the 'palace walls' is a significant reference to the result of the French Revolution whereby the proletariat in France had their 'blood' spilt as they attacked the barricades. Here, it appears as though Blake is sending a veiled warning to the ruling classes of Britain that this could happen again should the working classes remain shackled. Furthermore, the conflict between those in power and those without power is reinforced through the image of the proletariat's 'mind-forged manacles'. In particular, the idea that the 'manacles' are only 'forged' in the 'mind' could signify the way in which the lower classes could easily break free but seem to not know how to.

The idea of those who are powerless being bound to those in power is presented to us by Tennyson in his poem *The Charge of the Light Brigade*. Tennyson writes that the light brigade had no say in what happened, instead being told that 'their [mission was] but to do and die'. Specifically, the connective 'and' reveals that should the light brigade act, they would meet their untimely fate. This is something that Blake also references within *London* as he demonstrates that those in poverty also had relatively little control over their destiny through his continual use of juxtaposition. This is exemplified when he includes ideas such as the 'harlot's curse' that 'blasts the new born infant's tear', clearly revealing that the pure 'infant' would be subjected to the dark depths of society if those with power chose to continue, as Tennyson writes, 'blunder'.

> There is continual weaving of ideas in this paragraph between the two poems. This allows for an exploratory approach to be taken.

Control exerted on the citizens of London, and London itself as a place, is expertly conveyed by Blake through his opening repetition of the adjective 'chartered'. Not only does Blake refer to the 'chartered street' where it appears that inhabitants are funnelled through controlled pathways, but he also conveys the image of the ruling classes' attempts to control even the most natural sources as he comments on the 'chartered Thames'. This image presents conflict in the way that a river cannot be completely controlled, which could potentially cause conflict between the river and those who wish to restrict it. Whilst the river may be confined by its banks and take a route that it has done for centuries, it is almost as though Blake attempts to comment on the fact that rivers do burst their banks and flooding does occur. This image of the 'chartered Thames' could potentially be metaphorical of the idea that whilst the proletariat may be confined by their own 'mind forged manacles' at present, that they may not be forever. This is yet another warning to echo his political allusion of the 'palace walls' to those who wish to take note and recognise the unharnessed power of those who feel unable to advocate for themselves.

> The candidate strongly shows that they understand the explicit choices that the poet makes. This analysis as the paragraph develops becomes critical as the images are closely examined. The candidate also links back to ideas that have been previously expressed.

Like the lack of power that the proletariat have within *London*, we need only look to the use of Tennyson's inclusion of specific voice in *The Charge of the Light Brigade* to acknowledge the conflict between the anonymised leader and the '600'. Tennyson uses speech within his poem "Forward, the Light Brigade! Charge for the guns!' he said' whereby the imperative verbs reveal the sense of direction and control that the leader (now widely believed to have been the voice of Lord Raglan) exerted over the light brigade. The conflict comes where the soldiers are not able to 'make reply' or 'question why' and instead are left to suffer in silence; to 'do and die'. It is this silencing of individuals that allows for a reader to understand the real conflict between those with power and those without. Whilst the 'hapless soldier' can only 'sigh' in *London* and the light brigade cannot 'question' their superiors, this conflict could easily erupt and pose potential problems in the future. This is something both Tennyson hints at with his recognition that the '600' are

> **How does the candidate successfully link back to the opening of their essay here to ensure cohesion?**

> Ideas are linked seamlessly together to conclude and leaves no doubt that the candidate fully understands the context of both poems.

controlled by one solo voice and a point that Blake more confidently makes through his images of the Thames and the French Revolution. The mass of the oppressed voices could overpower the smaller numbers of powerful voices if they are only shown how to.

Critical response

This is a critical response most notably because of the depth and development of the analysis within it. A confident introduction sets up strong ideas that are continually referred to throughout the essay. The analysis of language is incredibly detailed and very specific links are made across the two poems. All the candidate's ideas are laid firmly against a detailed understanding of the contexts of these two poems that cannot be ignored in poems that deal with conflict that have impacted upon history.

Place – *The Émigrée*

4.4 Compare how place is presented in *The Émigrée* by Carol Rumens and one other poem.

4.4.1 Critical response

About her relationships with a place, despite the fact she is now not in the place – 'my city hides behind me' – significance of a place, sacrifice herself for the place.	Nobody can change her memory of the place (unlike *The Prelude*) 'bright filled paperweight' metaphor + bright with semantic field
Power over place – mental impact Lasts long after we leave *The Prelude*: a trouble to my dreams *The Émigrée*: my memory of it is sunlight clear	Repetition emphasising place's impact *The Prelude*: huge peak black and huge *The Émigrée*: branded by an impression of sunlight, place something not physical

For both Wordsworth and Rumens' speakers, the impact of a place goes beyond the physical. Significantly, both poems portray place as having a long-lasting mental impact on an individual, and its impact lasting long after the speaker has left the place. Both poets are highlighting how humanity can have a relationship with the places we inhabit and how those relationships can have an impact on us mentally.

Rumens' speaker in *The Émigrée* presents her place as an almost human entity to establish the relationship she has with her homeland. In the final stanza, she begins exploring her relationship by personifying the 'city' and completing various actions with it. The city 'lies down' and the speaker begins to 'comb its hair', and later they go 'dancing together'. We might infer that the speaker has an almost maternal relationship with the city (much like Wordsworth's speaker's relationship with nature), which is interesting as she 'left it as a child'. Notably, there also seems to be a submissive element to the city, in lying 'down in front' of the speaker, it offers a sense of trust and welcomes the speaker's interaction. This loyalty is later emphasised in 'my city hides behind me', which offers the speaker as self-sacrificial and willing to put herself in danger with the ominous and ambiguous 'they' who 'circle' the speaker and the city. This almost dream-like interaction with the personified 'city' tells the reader that the speaker's relationship with the place is a permanent one, despite the fact she is no longer there. Rumens, therefore, establishes that a place, in this case a person's homeland, is somewhere that we never fully leave, perhaps physically, but never mentally.

Although *The Prelude* might not be an obvious choice to compare, the introduction sets up clear links between the two poems.

This first paragraph is consistent and detailed when it explores one idea.

Can you select any tentative (not certain) phrases used here? Why might these phrases be useful when exploring a poem like *The Émigrée*?

This opening point links back well to the overview provided at the start. The response is building an argument rather than giving a series of separate ideas.

Notably, the émigrée's relationship with her place cannot be affected once she has left. She describes her memory of the place as something that 'cannot break' and describes it as a 'bright, filled paperweight'. This metaphor establishes that the place is almost a physical object that she can carry with her, and even if people do attempt to break it, they can't – the metaphor of the 'paperweight' hints that it's almost made of reinforced glass – and will permanently be fixed. Moreover, we could consider this metaphor to imply that the impact of her native country is something that mentally grounds her, or holds her down, like the purpose of a 'paperweight'. The adjective 'bright' suggests that the paperweight is flooded with light, which is structurally reinforced throughout the poem, as the motif of light is used to associate her homeland with positivity. We are told in the second line that her 'memory' of the place is 'sunlight-clear', and later it has 'white' streets and a 'white plane' with 'sunlight' used throughout the poem. This motif reassures the reader that no matter what darkness has taken over her home country, she will always remember it in a positive light. For her, it is consumed by 'sunlight', unlike in *The Prelude*, where he is consumed by 'darkness'. Perhaps Rumens is telling us that it is not the place that has an impact on individuals but instead the memory that we hold of it and how that affects us once we have left.

Both Wordsworth and Rumens present places that have a mental impact on their speakers, one that they either don't wish to, or can't, fully escape. In *The Émigrée*, we quickly learn that her 'memory of it is sunlight clear', and in the final line of *The Prelude* the speaker tells us the place has become 'a trouble to my dreams'. Here we can establish that for both speakers, the memory of the place has had a lasting impact on them and has caused some sort of alteration in perspective. These impacts are evidently very different: Wordsworth's speaker has now a negative relationship as he leaves feeling 'grave and serious', contrasting Rumens' speaker's positive perspective on her unbroken 'original view'. Interestingly, both speakers take possession of each place, with the possessive pronoun 'my' being used to highlight their intense, individual relationships with the place. But, of course, for Wordsworth, contextually, we know that his relationship with nature was far more complex than one single moment of feeling threatened, with his other Romantic poems highlighting his admiration and awareness of the world and the power of nature. In this particular extract from the much longer poem, the impact becomes 'darkness' rather than the 'sunlight' repeated to us by Rumens. So, whilst both Wordsworth and Rumens establish the long-lasting impact of a place, each of them offers the reader with a different kind of impact. Either way, there is the sense that a place will not leave us mentally, even if we leave it physically.

Each poet places emphasis on the mental impact of the place in a similar way. Both Wordsworth and Rumens utilise repetition to accentuate how each place targets the speakers' emotions. Whilst in *The Prelude* this repetition is isolated

How does this paragraph explore the different meanings created by a single metaphor? How are these ideas linked across the poem, beyond the metaphor?

This evidence is selected in order to support the response, and well-integrated into the paragraph.

There is a sustained comparison of the two texts, with the response moving between the poems.

How has the candidate used historical context well here and integrated it into the response?

to one crucial line describing the 'huge peak, black and huge', in *The Émigrée* the repetition is patterned throughout the poem with the use of 'sunlight' throughout to return us to the place's positive impact. Beginning with *The Prelude*, the repeated simplistic adjective 'huge' spotlights the loss of articulation for Wordsworth, his earlier eloquent language describing nature 'glittering idly in the moon' and the peak as 'the horizon's utmost boundary' is now reduced to the monosyllabic 'huge peak'. Here, the place has had an impact on Wordsworth in a very immediate sense, as it affects his ability to communicate the sheer magnitude of nature. This contrasts to Rumens' use of 'sunlight'. Structurally, each stanza ends with 'sunlight', creating a repeated cycle of the place having a positive impact, despite the negative connotations established in each stanza. Each stanza contains the negatives of the place, such as 'tyrants', 'banned by the state' and 'they circle me', but ultimately, we return to the 'sunlight' – and this structural repetition serves to establish how the place will last in her memory as an unbroken place of flooding light. Both Rumens and Wordsworth create places which have mentally impacted their speakers, and for both, with time passed, they are unable to change that memory. Of course, Rumens' speaker does not want to change her unbreakable 'paperweight' memory, whereas Wordsworth's speaker struggles to reconcile his new version of the landscape with his old one.

> Being able to closely compare the effects of similar methods shows excellent understanding of the two poems.

> **What vocabulary is used by the candidate in this paragraph to ensure the analysis sounds sophisticated and mature?**

> These closing lines of the final paragraph are a bringing together of all the ideas so far which have proved the opening argument.

Critical response

This essay is exploratory, particularly due to its sound understanding of both poems. It is evident that the candidate knows both poems extremely well, evidenced through the seamless integration of evidence and the close comparisons which are drawn out. The response uses subject terminology as a way to enhance their understanding of the meanings created by each poet, ensuring detailed and sophisticated analysis throughout.

Power – *My Last Duchess*

4.5 Compare how power is presented in *My Last Duchess* by Robert Browning and one other poem.

4.5.1 Critical response

Duchess whilst silent exerts and controls the duke's actions and words to others	WP is silent in what he says, and instead allows his pictures to say what he cannot	WP recognises the limits of his own voice, whilst the duke believes her silence is representative of her lack of power (which it is not).
'none puts by the curtain I have drawn for you but I' Skill in speech – which I do not	'In his dark room he is finally alone... like a priest preparing to intone a mass'	
'Let herself be lessoned so' 'I gave commands then all smiles stopped'	Sought approval to do what someone must Readers' eyeballs prick with tears	

How does the candidate immediately narrow the focus of the question?

How could the candidate ensure that all ideas here are fully explained?

The candidate fluently expresses ideas linked to the question and their overall argument.

Power comes in many forms, but the quiet power of silence can quite often be underestimated. Within both *My Last Duchess* and *War Photographer*, the subjects of the poems display their respective unobtrusive power through the way in which they silently communicate with those whom they most want to.

Quite commonly believed to be powerful and dominant, the duke – the poem's voice – within *My Last Duchess* opens his dramatic monologue with the line 'That's my last Duchess painted on the wall / Looking as if she were alive'. The deictic reference 'that's' ensures that the duke has control over his listener within the poem as it is clear that he is referring to a specific 'painted' image that they can both see. The duke uses the focal point of the painting to attempt to convey the power that he holds over his 'last' duchess to the emissary, yet little does he realise that the act of him positioning her as a work of art only serves to elevate the control that she silently exerts over him. The duke attempts to endear himself to the emissary as he comments that 'Even had you skill In speech—which I have not', which only serves to demonstrate that he fails to recognise what he does throughout. Not only does he clearly believe himself to be a successful speaker – we never hear from the emissary as the entire poem is written in the form of a dramatic monologue, but he also fails to recognise that his words, like his actions, hold very little power. After all, he is only speaking to an emissary and not anyone of real significance. It is little wonder that he holds court with them; his voice is less powerful than the lack of voice of the duchess.

The duke comments that 'none puts by the curtain I have drawn for you but I' where our attention must be given to his assertion that it is his action; 'I have drawn'. Interestingly, this use of action is shown to be in the past tense that could potentially signify that his power, like his actions, is also left within the past. It is the act of him keeping his duchess as an artefact that shows his distinct lack of power. Whilst many may believe that he has the ultimate power as he 'gave commands', this action is only required because he was not able to control her in the way in which he would have liked whilst she 'were alive'. Not only does the duke fail to erase all memories of the duchess, but he also keeps her painted on the wall as a relic and 'puts by the curtain' to share her with others – they very thing he wanted to avoid. This is surely testament to the power of the duchess' silence in that she no longer needs to even communicate with him to be valued. Most importantly, whilst the painting may fade, she is a permanent fixture in the duke's life for as long as he chooses her to be.

Silent power is also a key theme that is present within Carol Ann Duffy's *War Photographer*. The poem opens with the line 'In his dark room he is finally alone' where particular attention must be paid to the adverb 'finally' as it is almost as if he has been waiting for space and silence to fulfil his 'job', which suggests just how powerful silence is for the photographer's ability to work. Linked to this is the biblical image of him being in 'a church and he a priest preparing to intone a Mass'. In a similar fashion to the duchess, the photographer's quiet power is seen through his comparison of himself to a priest. Churches are commonly viewed as quiet and serious settings with priests being charged with the blessing and the looking after of both the living and the dead. Whilst the power of this role could be seen to be somewhat overlooked, the comparison allows for a reader to recognise the value and power that his role in the development of these photographs holds.

Whilst not in 'rural England', we are told how the photographer 'sought approval without words to do what someone must', again signifying the power that silence has albeit in a slightly different way. The photographer cannot communicate with the subjects of his photographs verbally. This could be because there may be no time to do so or, more simply, because of a language barrier. Moreover, the power of the photographer is in his role itself and not in the language that he uses to discuss his role. He can silently carry out his 'job' showing the importance that it carries. It is the opposite scenario within *My Last Duchess* however, in that the duke must use his voice to carry out his will as he 'gave commands'. Whilst the duke is confident to tell the emissary of all of the duchess' misgivings, his use of deliberately ambiguous language when he explains that 'he gave commands then all smiles stopped' leaves a reader questioning how these 'smiles stopped' and why the duke felt that he needed to go to such extreme lengths in order to gain silence, which only leads to allowing the duchess more power than she potentially held in the first place.

Some very detailed pieces of analysis are explored in this paragraph which are supported by a thorough understanding of the text conveyed through well-embedded quotations.

How has the candidate used imagery here to explore ideas that support their response?

The links in this paragraph are subtle allowing the candidate to focus on the second poem.

The candidate recognises the nuances within the poem and links to the overall response.

Can you identify how the candidate not only compares ideas here, but also links back to ideas expressed previously in the essay?

The close of this essay links all the explored ideas together in order to conclude successfully.

Whilst the subjects within both poems clearly recognise the impact that both their silence and their voice can have, it is undeniable that the poets offer them the opportunity to use their voices. The significance of silence, however, is truly appreciated through examining the role that the photographer plays; he 'must' share his images and through the recognition that silence carries an unacknowledged power within *My Last Duchess*, we see the duke's self-perceived power fading through every calculated line he speaks.

Critical response

This essay shows the power of a candidate who narrows the focus of a wide question so that they can build a response and argument that is detailed and precise. This response is critical as it acknowledges the nuances in the power of silence and does so through judicious selection of evidence to support ideas. The response feels heavily lead by the analysis of *My Last Duchess* but the points that are made about *War Photographer* are specific and serve to complement those made about *My Last Duchess*.

Regret – *Poppies*

4.6 Compare how ideas about regret are presented in *Poppies* by Jane Weir and one other poem.

4.6.1 Critical response

Within both *Poppies* and *Remains* by Simon Armitage, the central voices of the poems express their sense of regret that is linked to the different conflicts in which they are involved, either directly or indirectly. Within *Remains*, we see the soldier struggle as he never gets to the 'end of [the] story'; his memories of regret haunt his days. In comparison to this, the mother in *Poppies* is indirectly affected by war as her son has chosen to leave to play a role within it and we are left with a figure of a solitary woman who longs to 'hear [his] playground voice catching on the wind'. Although told from different perspectives – one from a soldier and one from a civilian, both poems depict the regret that these figures face potentially because of the powerlessness that they felt at the time the action took place.

A clear sense of the soldier's memories haunting him are ever-present within *Remains*. The poem, composed of two distinct parts, presents the reader with a sense that the soldier along with 'somebody else and somebody else' will never be free of the memory of their actions and thus endure a keen sense of regret even when 'home on leave'. The central voice comments that 'his blood shadow stays on the street' whereby a reader almost gets the impression that this is not an isolated event. The use of the third person possessive pronoun 'his' is seen to anonymise the 'looter', suggesting that this act of 'letting fly' happened in a momentary second where no real attention was paid to the man that had been 'sent out/to tackle'. Perhaps this is where a real sense of regret stems from; the men were powerless to take the time to question those orders that would have come to them so quickly. Furthermore, this suggestion that the soldier's regret will haunt him is seen through the disturbing image of the 'blood shadow'. Specifically, the noun 'shadow' alludes to something created by man – an impression created by blocking light. Despite a shadow only being visible in 'broad daylight', a shadow is always present no matter what. Coupled with the adjective 'blood', there is a sense that this soldier will always be tainted and followed by the blood of another. It is almost as though Armitage is drawing our attention to the fact that, whilst men may regret their actions and are left forced to live with them, they are unable to change what happened due to their powerlessness in a volatile war zone.

The inability to change the position that one finds themselves in is an idea that is also portrayed within *Poppies*. The mother is powerless to influence her

> This opening expresses the candidate's response to the question thoughtfully and fluently.

> **Can you identify the structure the candidate has used to present their ideas in the introduction for clarity?**

> **Can you identify the tentative language that is used to suggest meanings created within the poem?**

> Careful development of ideas through short sentences allows for sophistication to be built carefully so that ideas do not become muddled or confused.

> **Can you identify how cohesion has been built across the paragraphs here?**

son's decision to go to war, yet she still holds on to every memory that she can savour to minimise any regrets that she may be left with once he departs. This is seen in the mother's actions as she 'pinned [a poppy] onto [his] lapel', which could be seen to be her way of marking her son as she attaches this symbol of remembrance onto him; a potential act designed to ensure that she too is remembered. The mother cannot change her son's mind over his decision to go to war and she directly references the idea that she believes that he has been indoctrinated into leaving. Stating that 'you were away, intoxicated' shows the extent to which she feels as if he has been altered by ideas that he has ingested. Weir's decision to include the verb 'intoxicated', as opposed to a more colloquial alternative such as drunk, subtly suggests a sense of being poisoned, which could reveal that the mother regrets that her son has grown up and no longer listens solely to her but instead to others who now appear to exert a greater influence over him.

Interestingly, *Poppies* is told solely from the viewpoint of the mother, and we have no indication of how the son responds to her other than that he has left. It could be suggested that the mother may regret not directly speaking to her son about how she truly feels. She comments that the world is 'overflowing like a treasure chest' where this simile is a familiar image from adventure stories read by children. However, like a child, the son still holds onto the idea that treasure awaits him, whilst the mother recognises the limitations of searching for this fabled 'chest' that she knows will not contain what it promises.

Lost promises and ideas about what may happen are also present within *Remains*. Following the volta, the soldier states that he's 'home on leave. But I blink and he bursts again through the door of the bank'. The soldier struggles to compartmentalise the images of war when he returns home and cannot 'leave' them in the 'sun smothered land'. Instead, the caesura acknowledges that despite the break in service, the image returns to him and it is not the 'end of story' he hoped for. The use of the metaphor 'he's here dug in behind enemy lines' reinforces the idea that this is an intrusive image which crosses a boundary potentially revealing the idea that his image of the looter becomes inextricably bound with him due to the deep sense of regret that he feels. The soldier slowly begins to understand that the looter is not 'left for dead' and understands that he must live with the repercussions of his actions.

In a different light, the mother within *Poppies* never fully accepts what has happened unlike the soldier. Whilst she states that she 'released a song bird from its cage', which could be metaphorical of her letting her son leave, or could alternatively represent the inner anguish that she uncages, she doesn't fully let go. At the end of the poem, we learn of her 'hoping to hear [his] playground voice catching on the wind' in a sad moment of recognition that she has not fully let go, and potentially regrets leaving things unsaid. The volatility of a war zone is reflected in the domestic environment presented within *Poppies* whereby the mother feels the fragility of her son's situation. Just as the soldier in *Remains* feels that he is left suffering the view of the 'image of agony' – he has sacrificed the life of another due to his role and situation – this situation is reflected in a different way within *Poppies* as the mother is unable to protect her son from war and the unspoken sacrifice that she may feel he is making.

Critical response

This is a response that carefully builds in detail to lead to strong conclusions based on thoughtful analysis. What the candidate successfully does here is shows how regret is presented but from two very different voices. This is achieved through both language and structural analysis. Ideas are developed as the essay progresses and there is a real sense of cohesion throughout the paragraphs. It is the detail and confidence with the poems that ensures that this is a critical response.

Acknowledgements

This book would not have been possible had I not had the privilege of working with the best English teacher I've ever met. Laura, you reignited my love for teaching and challenge me to be the best teacher I can be. Your generosity, kindness and friendship are seen by myself, our colleagues and the students every day and I feel very lucky to have the relationship that we do. Thank you.

There are so many teachers who have supported me throughout my career that I could never thank them all. However, I give my sincere thanks to our most trusted friend and colleague, Rebecca whose kind and honest feedback has been so very valuable and appreciated.

Whilst he will insist that he has had nothing to do with this book, I must also thank our headteacher, Dave who allows his staff to believe in themselves immeasurably. This faith in me, and us, means that projects like this can be believed in.

My parents always encouraged me to pursue my dreams. Without them, I would not have the resilience and passion that I do; I am grateful for the love that they continue to shower me with. I hope this book makes you both very proud.

Gareth, without your love and belief, I would not push myself to do things that, at first, seem impossible. You are my biggest champion and I am so grateful that you support me unreservedly.

Finally, thank you to the students who I have taught and have yet to teach. I hope this book helps you to realise that you can achieve beyond your wildest dreams and pursue everything that you set your mind to.

Becky Jones

To all the students I teach or have taught: for helping me to explore the depths of every text I teach, giving me half of these ideas (just kidding...), and for making every lesson fresh and exciting. I hope this book will be useful to those I teach in the future.

To all of the wonderful people I work with: for being an amazing team of wonderful humans and for constantly making me think and want to be the best teacher I can possibly be. To Dave for being a leader who embraces perfectionism and never accepting me at less than my best. To Rebecca for being the only eye we could let scrutinise and pre-read because we trust her insight and kindness. I hope this book will help us to keep getting better.

To all the ones I love: for accepting my love for my career, for always being there when it gets tough, and for allowing me to pursue everything in all the desperate obsession that fuels me. To my sister for always putting the fire in me, to my nan and mum for teaching me what it is to be an empowered and strong woman. To Darren, for being superhuman, and for making every minute of my day possible. I hope this book will make you all proud.

To Becky, of course, because what would this book be without you? It wouldn't exist. Thank you for making me fall in love with teaching all over again, for teaching me what it is to be a fearless leader, and for being the cleverest person I know. I couldn't imagine anyone better to finally see my name in print next to. I hope this book is only the beginning.

And to Jude. Because it always is, and always will be, for you.

Laura Webb